A Guide to
Tactical Planning

A Guide to Tactical Planning

Producing Your Short-Term Results

George L. Morrisey

Jossey-Bass Publishers • San Francisco

Substantial discounts on bulk quantities of Jossey-Bass books are
available to corporations, professional associations, and other
organizations. For details and discount information, contact the
special sales department at Jossey-Bass Inc., Publishers.
(415) 433-1740; Fax (800) 605-2665.

For sales outside the United States, please contact your local
Simon & Schuster International Office.

Manufactured in the United States of America.

Library of Congress Cataloging-in-Publication Data

Morrisey, George L.
    Morrisey on planning : a guide to tactical planning : producing your
short-term results / George L. Morrisey.
        p.   cm. — (Jossey-Bass business and management series)
    Includes bibliographical references and index.
    ISBN 0-7879-0170-9
    1. Strategic planning.   I. Title.   II. Series.
HD30.28.M654   1996
658.4'012—dc20   95-23792
                                                                          CIP

FIRST EDITION
HB Printing   10   9   8   7   6   5   4   3   2   1

THE JOSSEY-BASS BUSINESS AND MANAGEMENT SERIES

THE
MORRISEY ON PLANNING
SERIES

A Guide to Strategic Thinking
Building Your Planning Foundation

A Guide to Long-Range Planning
Creating Your Strategic Journey

A Guide to Tactical Planning
Producing Your Short-Term Results

Contents

CHAPTER THREE
What's Your Focus?
Determining Your Unit's Key Results Areas   27

CHAPTER FOUR
What's Important?
Identifying and Analyzing Your Critical Issues   33

Introduction to the Series

My experience in working with the planning process over a period of many years with a wide variety of client organizations has led me to the conclusion that there are three phases managers must go through in this process, each characterized by a distinctly different mind-set. The first phase is *strategic thinking*, which focuses on the more *intuitive* aspects of the process leading to the development of the organization's mission, vision, and strategy. This phase is designed to create the organization's future *perspective* while establishing a foundation from which all major planning decisions will be made.

The second phase is *long-range planning*, which calls for a combination of intuitive and *analytical* thinking leading to projections of future *positions* the organization wishes to attain. This phase is designed to validate and activate the mission, vision, and strategy created during the first phase.

The third phase is *tactical planning*, which is primarily an analytical approach with some intuitive overtones that leads to specific actions affecting the organization's current *performance*. This phase is designed to produce the short-term results needed to carry out the organization's mission and to reach the future positions that have been projected.

I have established this three-book series to reflect how several of my clients have chosen to work through the planning process. By design, the books are

- Short, practical, and how-to oriented. They are a length that is more comfortable for most managers than many of the longer, more theoretical books on the subject.

- Easily portable and appropriate for introspective reading during quiet times (such as on an airplane trip).

- Designed as an interrelated series, yet each book stands on its own as a guide to doing a more effective job on the aspect of planning addressed in that particular book.

- Useful source materials for seminars and workshops on planning; they also may be used as pre-reading and advance assignments for facilitated planning events and as ongoing reference books for individual managers and management teams as they work with the process on the job.

The first book, *A Guide to Strategic Thinking: Building Your Planning Foundation,* will help you get your planning team started by determining your organization's principles and values as well as the strategic direction in which you should be moving. While there is heavier emphasis in this book on the roles of the CEO and the senior management team, it provides guidance for all managers throughout your organization who must contribute to the strategic planning process.

The second book, *A Guide to Long-Range Planning: Creating Your Strategic Journey,* provides the tools for establishing a focus on the positions toward which your organization needs to strive in such areas as future markets, future products and services, technology, human competencies, and financial projections. It will be useful for all managers in your organization who need to focus on the future.

The third book, *A Guide to Tactical Planning: Producing Your Short-Term Results,* will provide all managers (executives, middle managers, first-line supervisors, and individual contributors alike) with a methodology for achieving meaningful short-term results on both a planned and an ad hoc basis.

The brief nature of each book makes this series a resource that participating managers can easily use on an ongoing basis as well as in preparing for formal planning efforts. While the emphasis in each use will be different, all managers have a vested interest in making both the strategic and tactical planning processes work in their areas of responsibility. All of the books contain examples drawn from individual departments and work units as well as from the perspective of the total organization. Some of these examples are identified as coming from specific organizations with which I have worked. Others represent adaptations from the efforts of organizations I have chosen not to identify. All of the examples are real.

As with any set of tools, the effective use of these books is dependent upon the desire and skill of the person using them. They are not designed as a substitute for sound managerial judgment. Rather, they are intended to enhance that judgment in order to help you and other managers in your organization do a more consistent and creative job of planning to meet future as well as current needs. Best wishes in your journey!

Acknowledgments

I have been privileged to be associated with many of the top management thinkers of our time. They have significantly influenced my work, as resources and in many cases as direct collaborators. They include, of course, my two previous coauthors of Jossey-Bass publications—*The Executive Guide to Strategic Planning* and *The Executive Guide to Operational Planning*—Patrick Below and Betty Acomb, as well as Bonnie Abney, Louis Allen, N. H. Atthreya, Joe Batten, Arthur Beck, Fred Clark, Donn Coffee, Tom Connellan, Peter Drucker, Marie Kane, Alec Mackenzie, Bob Mager, Dale McConkey, Henry Migliore, Howard Mold, George Odiorne, Gene Seyna, Brian Tracy, and Glenn Varney.

I am especially appreciative of the many fine managers within the organizations I have served as a consultant, who have allowed me the opportunity to validate the concepts and techniques of effective planning while providing me with excellent feedback that helped immeasurably in refinement of the process. I would like particularly to acknowledge two outstanding managers who have demonstrated how this process can work effectively over a long period of time in a variety of increasingly responsible positions: Chris Ellefson of BHP Minerals International and Nelson Marchioli of Burger King.

I have been blessed to be associated for several years with a group of professional speakers, trainers, and consultants that we, its members, refer to as our mentor group. These colleagues have encouraged, critiqued, and otherwise helped me to hone my ideas and to properly position my publications as well as my services to clients. They are Tom Callister, Lola Gillebaard, Jane Holcomb, Eileen McDargh, Jack Mixner, and Karen Wilson.

Finally, but far from least, I will be eternally grateful for the continuous support I receive from my business partner, my best friend, and my loving wife for many years, Carol Morrisey.

Merritt Island, Florida   G.L.M.
April 1995

Preface

Portions of the present book were originally published in my earlier books on Management by Objectives and Results (MOR), as well as in a more recent book, *The Executive Guide to Operational Planning* (with Patrick J. Below and Betty L. Acomb, 1987). Both the title and the principal focus of the latter book implied that operational, or tactical, planning took place primarily at the upper levels of management. Many clients and readers liked the approach but wanted something that could be used as a guide by managers at *all* levels of the organization, since in reality most planning takes place at the lower levels. The focus of the present book, therefore, is primarily on how middle and first-level managers can use the planning process to manage their respective organizational units, while at the same time it retains the concepts and techniques that senior managers can put to work in establishing plans for the entire organization.

In addition to the modification in thrust, I have made some other refinements to the steps in the tactical planning process based on extensive experience in working with a wide range of client organizations from high-tech organizations to manufacturing companies to retail operations to service organizations to government agencies and other not-for-profit groups. For example, I discovered in working with some client organizations that determining Key Results Areas *before* going through Critical Issue Analysis, whether at the unit or total organization level, provided a better focus for identifying and addressing those issues that will have a major impact on the organization's work during the coming year. I have also expanded the use of Critical Issue Analysis as an ongoing technique for dealing with issues or problems whenever they arise, not just during the formation of plans.

Indicators of Performance have been changed to Key Performance Indicators (KPIs) because this terminology seems to communicate the concept better to many managers. I have established a separate chapter on this step of the process and have added emphasis on its importance in determining what should be measured. And finally, I have added a chapter on Plan Review, updated and adapted from my MOR books, which provides unit managers with concepts and techniques they can use to both monitor and modify their plans as they proceed with implementing them.

While many organizations continue to use and benefit from the processes presented in my earlier books, I believe that this version will be even more useful, particularly for those managers who work "in the trenches."

How Can This Book Be Used?

There are several ways you can use this book—for instance, as a

- Guide for management teams preparing their annual plans at both the total organization and unit levels.
- Guide for individual managers and management teams in their ongoing tactical planning efforts.
- Text for an in-house workshop on planning skills for managers. The book is laid out in a logical manner that lends itself to a segmented instructional plan.
- Text for a college or university extension program or a public seminar on planning skills for managers. (Note: the content and examples are directed primarily toward participants who wish to apply it in their own work areas, not toward those studying management theory.)

- Reference guide for internal and external consultants charged with helping organizations and managers with their planning efforts.

- Individual study guide for the working manager or prospective manager.

For self-study, I recommend the following approach:

1. Read the Preface and Chapters One, Two, and Nine for an overview of the planning philosophy and process being presented.

2. Determine which of the following alternatives best serves your individual needs:

    a. Selective learning of specific techniques to supplement your existing knowledge

    b. Concentrating on learning the objective-setting and action-planning steps for use in your individual or unit efforts

    c. Concentrating on learning the critical issue analysis process as an ongoing problem-solving approach

    d. Learning and applying the entire process to your job

3. If you have selected 2(a) as most appropriate for you, the recommendation is easy: study and practice those steps that will satisfy your needs.

4. If 2(b) seems best for you at the moment, Chapters Six and Seven will be of most value to you. I recommend that you identify one major work effort that would be suitable for initial application of this approach. Then, following the guidelines given, write out the objective(s) and action plan(s) required to accomplish it. Concentrating on only one major effort will give you an opportunity to learn from the experience, after which the application of the entire tactical planning process can be further expanded as desired.

5. If 2(c) looks intriguing, go through Chapter Four. Then, take a particularly thorny problem (or opportunity) and work

through the analysis process with your team or as an individual. Resist the temptation to jump too quickly to the "solution" since the process may open some alternatives you had not previously considered. Also, you may discover that you are analyzing the wrong issue and a clarification may occur.

6. If you are ready to commit yourself to 2(d), I suggest reading the Appendix, "Developing Unit Roles and Missions," to determine if that might be an appropriate starting point for your unit. If you are satisfied with your current mission statement, I recommend defining your Key Results Areas first in order to segment areas in which your planning efforts need to be focused. Then proceed selectively through the rest of the process in a few key areas of work effort, gradually working the approach into the entire job.

7. Use the book as a continual reference, particularly Chapters Four and Nine and the various working tools and checklists, as you continue your application of this tactical planning process.

8. Don't get discouraged when you hit the inevitable periods of setback and frustration in application of this approach to planning. Stay with the process, and both your satisfaction and your effectiveness will increase as you continue to develop your skill.

Get ready now to become an even more effective manager than you already are through the use of this practical, proven approach to tactical planning!

Merritt Island, Florida　　　　　　　　　　　　　　　　　　　　G.L.M.
August 1995

The Author

George L. Morrisey is chairman of The Morrisey Group, a management consulting firm based in Merritt Island, Florida. He received his B.S. (1951) and M.Ed. (1952) from Springfield College. He has more than twenty years of experience as a practicing manager and key specialist with such organizations as the YMCA, First Western Bank, Rockwell International, McDonnell Douglas, and the U.S. Postal Service, as well as more than twenty years as a full-time consultant, professional speaker, and seminar leader. He has personally assisted more than two hundred business, industrial, service, governmental, and not-for-profit organizations throughout the world in the areas of strategic and tactical planning.

Morrisey is the author or coauthor of fifteen books prior to this series, including *Management by Objectives and Results in the Public Sector* (1976); *Management by Objectives and Results for Business and Industry* (1977); *Getting Your Act Together: Goal Setting for Fun, Health and Profit* (1980); *Performance Appraisals for Business and Industry* (1983); *Performance Appraisals in the Public Sector* (1983); *The Executive Guide to Operational Planning* (with Patrick J. Below and Betty L. Acomb, 1987); *The Executive Guide to Strategic Planning* (with Patrick J. Below and Betty L. Acomb, 1987); *Effective Business and Technical Presentations* (with Thomas L. Sechrest, 1987); and *Creating Your Future: Personal Strategic Planning for Professionals* (1992). He is the author and producer of several learning programs on audiocassette and videocassette, all directed toward helping individuals and organizations become more effective and self-fulfilled.

A professional's professional, Morrisey received the Certified Speaking Professional (CSP) designation in 1983 and was recognized in 1984 with the CPAE (Council of Peers Award for Excellence), the highest recognition granted to a professional speaker by the National Speakers Association. In addition, in 1994, Morrisey was the sixteenth annual recipient of the Cavett Award, named in honor of the founder of the National Speakers Association, Cavett Robert. Morrisey is a former member of the boards of directors of the Association for Management Excellence (originally the International MBO Institute) and the National Speakers Association.

For further information on Morrisey's services, please contact:

The Morrisey Group
P.O. Box 541296
Merritt Island, FL 32954-1296
(800) 535-8202, (407) 452-7414, Fax (407) 452-2129

MORRISEY ON PLANNING

A Guide to Tactical Planning

CHAPTER ONE

Who Does the Planning? You, That's Who!

Why Plan? Results, That's Why!

Planning is not "them," it's "us." Planning is not something that happens "to us," it happens "by us" in every organization that achieves meaningful and consistent results. Planning is an essential part of every manager's job. Please note that *manager* has a small *m*. It is not a title or a position in an organization. A manager is anyone who has responsibility for the use of resources, which can range from millions of dollars and hundreds of people to how you use your own time and energy. My definition of management is *the effective use of limited resources to achieve desired results*. The purpose of this book, as well as the other two in this series, is to help you increase your own effectiveness as a manager by strengthening your planning skills and building on what is already working effectively for you. This particular book focuses on tactical, short-term, or what is sometimes referred to as annual, planning. Some of the concepts and techniques in this book will represent familiar territory for you while others will provide additional managerial insights. Since this book is designed to satisfy the needs of both experienced managers/planners and those relatively new to the process, please forgive my covering some of the basics.

What Is the Unit President Concept?

One way of approaching tactical planning is to use the Unit President concept that was introduced in the previous volumes in this series. Whether you are CEO of your organization, a division or department head, a middle manager, a first-line supervisor, or an individual contributor within a larger unit, consider yourself as president of a company. Consider everyone else within the organization with whom you must relate, including your boss, as your board of directors. The responsibility of the president is to clearly identify the results the board needs and wants and to deliver them. Generally, presidents who consistently do this are allowed to manage their companies virtually any way they want within certain legal and organizational limits. This principle as well as the rest of the contents in this book are equally applicable whether you function as a manager in private enterprise, government, or a not-for-profit organization.

What Is Cross-Functional Management?

Okay, so you are president of your own company. Picture yourself as heading a subsidiary company within a larger organization. As such, you must work cooperatively with other subsidiaries to help achieve the overall results required. To do this, you need to understand what those "overall results" are so that you can determine what is an appropriate contribution for you to make. You also need to know what your fellow companies' plans are, and they need to know yours, so you can work together for the common good. This way of working does not mean that you lose your own identity in the process; it does, however, acknowledge that interdependence is needed among such companies. Cross-functional management means that, of necessity, most managers must impact the performance of other departments and that they in turn will be similarly impacted.

In other words, plans are a major form of communication within and among organizations with common interests. They are a means whereby you can reach agreement with others on your mutual expectations. They incorporate both strategic and tactical planning. I will describe these approaches in Chapter Two, with particular emphasis on tactical planning, which is the primary focus of this book.

Why Should *All* Managers Be Involved?

What are the benefits to both the organization and the people involved in following the planning processes described in these books?

• *Better results.* Individual and team involvement in and commitment to a plan produces better results nearly every time. If one person or group creates a plan and hands it to another person or group for implementation, you may get *compliance*—as a condition of continued employment—but you will rarely see *commitment.* Compliance usually results in minimal performance—people will do what has to be done, but not much more; commitment tends to produce optimal performance. Performance from *committed* people results in a tremendous return on investment compared to the cost of involvement.

• *Better plans.* When key people assess what is really *achievable*, more realistic plans will be established and, more important, carried out successfully. If you are a field manager, a systems engineer, or a quality assurance supervisor, you know better than anyone else what is really required to assure success in your areas of responsibility.

• *Better accountability.* If your key employees are involved in and committed to the development of your plans, it will be clear who is accountable for each action. Also, your employees will accept this accountability more readily if they have been involved in determining the content of the plan.

• *Better communication and coordination.* Your active involvement in the planning process leads to a clearer understanding of what is expected of you and of others. It also makes communication across organizational lines easier through a common frame of reference—the plan. Furthermore, if you have a vested interest in achieving specific objectives, you will quickly realize the value of your planning efforts when you have the support of your counterparts in other parts of the organization. In most situations, the best way to get support from someone else is to give them what they need and want from you. That's a "win-win" approach!

Why Do Many Managers Resist Becoming Involved?

Involvement and commitment do not come naturally to everyone. Here are some typical reactions from those who may resist the process. Let's see what might have caused their resistance and what can be done about it.

- *"I hate meetings!"* We all feel like this periodically, when we think about the amount of time required for planning. However, this is less a resistance to meetings themselves than to meetings that are perceived as nonproductive. Most people involved in planning efforts are busy, productive people who see meetings that drag on interminably as keeping them from other, more important duties.

Effective planning does require a commitment of your time, part of which is spent in meetings for coordination and integration of plans to ensure that everyone is pulling in the same direction. You can increase the acceptance of meetings by ensuring that there are clear expectations of what will be accomplished, that all participants come prepared to contribute, and that the meetings themselves move crisply and are completed on time.

- *"Paper, paper, and more paper!"* Unfortunately, many people involved in planning feel like they are drowning in a sea of paper. Some people view planning primarily as filling out forms and writing reports. While a certain amount of paperwork is both inevitable and necessary, it can and should be controlled. Morrisey's Law states that *the utility of any planning document is in inverse relationship to its length.* The most frequently used planning document is likely to be no longer than a single sheet of paper. A complete plan, of course, is likely to be considerably longer than a single sheet; however, since most of the time you will be dealing only with pieces of the entire plan, the closer these "pieces" come to a single sheet, the more likely they are to be used.

Properly prepared written plans serve many important purposes, one of which is to provide you with a means for establishing and agreeing on performance expectations and assessing progress relative to those expectations. Paperwork can be kept under control by focusing on the vital few results required at each level.

• *"Why make plans? We never use them."* Unfortunately, we are all too familiar with organizations whose managers go through the annual ritual of preparing plans (maybe as a result of a planning "retreat") which are then duplicated, distributed throughout the organization, and promptly shoved in the bottom drawer while everyone gets back to work. Then, at the end of the year, they are pulled out, dusted off, and compared with actual performance. Perhaps, sometimes by sheer coincidence, there is some similarity between what was planned and what actually occurred. Often, however, actual accomplishments turn out to be quite different from what was projected.

Part of the reason for this dilemma is the dynamic nature of the environments in which we work and live. The purpose of planning is not to lock you into a predetermined course of action, but rather to provide you with a baseline from which plans may be modified or changed entirely when circumstances justify. The use of a *formal plan review* (a minimum of once per quarter) enables you to check progress and to address three primary questions:

1. What is going well and what can we learn from it?
2. What is not going well and what are we doing about it?
3. What is different now from what existed when the plan was created?

Plans may need to be adjusted depending on your answers to these questions.

• *"I can't control what others are going to do!"* It's frustrating to be held accountable for certain results when you may be at the mercy of other people over whom you have no control. For example, you might be a customer service manager who needs detailed information from the sales force to complete customer profiles designed to facilitate more responsive service. Members of the sales force, however, may be paid on commission and time spent gathering that information has to be taken from revenue-producing efforts. Do you sometimes find that your number one priority ends up being number thirty-two on another person's list of thirty-one? Is it any wonder that such a situation leads to a feeling of helplessness and frustration?

In today's complex world, we can and must impact the performance of other departments with which we have to work. While certain conflicts are inevitable, many can be avoided or minimized through the use of cross-functional team planning. In the previous example, had you as the customer service manager involved members of the sales force in the original development of the plan and helped them understand how this effort might result in increased sales, your customer profiles might be available in your database ahead of schedule.

Who Does What in Planning?

As was pointed out in the first two books in this series, the responsibility for the development and implementation of the *total* organization's plan lies with the chief executive officer (CEO), or whoever is designated as your organization's key decision maker, and the senior management team, which includes major department heads, one or two key staff advisers, and whoever will be guiding the planning process. All managers and key employees provide input to the senior team's decision-making process and, of course, need to prepare supporting plans for their own units. You, as unit president, need to determine where you fit and develop your own plans accordingly. Let's take a look at each of these roles.

- *The CEO* must demonstrate strong leadership if the plan is to be properly developed and implemented. Among other responsibilities, the CEO must ensure that the plan is supportive of the organization's strategic plan and that *cross-functional planning* takes place. Planning must address such cross-functional issues as profitability, new product development, customer service, and employee development. It may require the CEO to become a "benevolent dictator" at times to ensure that decisions are made and that the process does not become bogged down.

• *Senior planning team members* function in dual roles. If you are a member of this team, you need to recognize that you serve as an extension of the office of the CEO in the development of the total plan. It needs to be clearly understood that when you are working on the plan, you are representing the interests of the entire organization, not primarily those of your own function or program. Your second role is to provide leadership in the development and implementation of an effective plan within your areas of responsibility.

• *The planning process facilitator's* responsibilities may be carried out by a planning coordinator, an internal or external coach/facilitator, and/or a member of an internal planning staff. These responsibilities may include such activities as

Designing or modifying the planning process

Training/coaching managers involved in the planning process

Facilitating planning meetings

Establishing and monitoring the planning schedule

Coordinating and handling logistics of planning meetings

Documenting and distributing records of planning meetings as well as the plans themselves

• If you are a *middle manager,* you are responsible for the development, coordination, and implementation of plans for each of the units under your supervision and for ensuring that those unit plans support the total organization's plan. The various unit plans are pulled together to ensure horizontal as well as vertical coordination, reducing the likelihood of either duplication of effort or effort gap. In addition, you as a middle manager are responsible for interpreting higher-level plans throughout the units under your supervision.

• If you are a *first-line manager,* whose job may include certain one-person operations, you will also develop your own plans, following the process described in this book. Once again, remember that the Unit President concept applies regardless of where you are in the management hierarchy.

Can Planning Be Used for Team Building?

Your team normally consists of you and your direct reports, although at times it may include representatives of other units with which you work. You and your team members need to be working from a common frame of reference if you are to succeed. The planning process is a natural vehicle for team building. By having those who are most affected participate in your planning decisions, you receive the dual benefit of more realistic and accurate input and a greater sense of ownership in those who must carry out the decisions. The planning process also leads to greater mutual support among team members as they recognize and accept the need for working together toward common objectives.

A key to successful team building in the planning process lies in you, as the team leader, establishing an environment in which open, frank communication takes place. By focusing on the results your team needs to achieve, your team members are able to perceive the bigger organizational picture and where they fit in, both as individuals and as a team within the larger organization. The sharing of differing points of view, as well as the creative energy that is stimulated through active interchange, frequently results in significantly better plans and better follow-through in carrying out these plans. In addition, the bonding that frequently takes place through such an effort can have long-lasting effects on how members of the team function on an ongoing basis. This result is a prime example of why the planning *process* may be more valuable than the plans developed.

In Summary

The effectiveness of your organization's tactical plan and resulting performance to that plan is in direct proportion to the degree of involvement and commitment of you and other key people in the planning process. The benefits of involvement include:

- Better results
- Better plans
- Better accountability
- Better communication and coordination

A number of factors may keep you and others from becoming more involved in the planning process:

- Too many meetings
- Excessive paperwork
- Plans that are not used
- Feelings of frustration because of the lack of support from others

An important aspect of planning is team building. This is enhanced by a planning process that promotes

- Participation
- Open discussion
- Mutual agreement and support at all levels

The ongoing involvement and commitment of all key people in the organization to both the plan and the process is the principal cohesive ingredient required in the development and implementation of your plans. Chapter Two provides an overview of the process and how you can adapt it to your situation.

What? Planned Results, That's What!

How? Tactical Planning, That's How!

The process of management often can be placed on a continuum between two theoretical extremes, as illustrated in Figure 2.1. At one extreme we have Management by Activity and Reaction (MAR). This approach is best typified by the manager who comes to work without the slightest idea of what will happen that day. The first telephone call that comes in, the first crisis that occurs, or the person who shouts the loudest will dictate where effort will be directed. We see lots of activity going on, and a complete sense of exhaustion at the end of a ten- to twelve-hour day, but any results achieved that day are purely coincidental. At the other extreme, we have Professional Management (PM). This approach is illustrated by the "perfect" manager, who has things so well organized, who has anticipated problems so thoroughly that there is a contingency plan ready for any major crisis that might occur. Consequently, he or she can take that three-month trip around the world with complete assurance that business will flow smoothly during that period. Another way of describing this continuum is with Fire Fighting at the left and Fire Prevention at the right.

Actually, neither of these extremes exists in its purest sense. No one is so clairvoyant that they will never have to react to something that was not anticipated. Likewise, presumably no one is functioning in a position without at least some idea of the direction in which they should be going. Most of us operate somewhere along the continuum, with our particular location on it changing frequently. We would probably agree, however, that the closer we

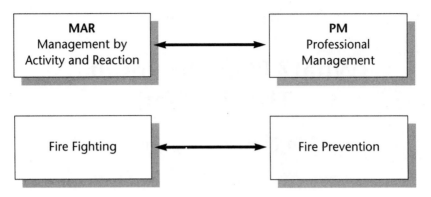

Figure 2.1 The Management Continuum

can come to the right end of the continuum, the more effective we are likely to be as managers. The process described in this book will help you move in that direction.

What Is Tactical Planning?

I remember seeing a comic strip one time that showed a football team in a huddle with a new quarterback giving instructions about the next play. He said, "On the third count, I will receive the ball at center, fake a handoff to Joe, fake a run to the right and then cut out around left end and up the sideline for a touchdown." As the team left the huddle to take their positions, one lineman turned to another and said, "You know, when I hear that third count and the ball is snapped, I'm going to stand up and watch. I don't want to miss any of that."

Whether we are playing a game of football or working to achieve worthwhile results on the job that will help carry out our mission, we are not going to "score a touchdown" unless we know where the goal line is and what it will take to get there, and unless everyone involved clearly understands and commits to doing their part to make the effort successful.

Tactical planning clearly defines what your organization or unit intends to accomplish, how and when this will take place, and who will be held accountable. It is also the means by which your portion of your organization's strategic plan is implemented.

Tactical planning has two separate parts—the plan and the process.

What Is a Tactical Plan?

Your *plan* is a document identifying specific results you need to achieve within a given period (usually one year). It also includes the specific actions and resources you need to accomplish these results. Six distinct elements make up the plan:

1. Key Results Areas
2. Critical Issue Analysis
3. Key Performance Indicators
4. Objectives
5. Action Plans
6. Plan Review

These elements and the processes involved in creating them will be discussed later in this and subsequent chapters.

What Is the Tactical Planning Process?

The planning *process* is the ongoing involvement of managers and key employees in producing plans and, more important, solid results for the total organization as well as for their individual units. As pointed out in Chapter One, a particular strength of this process is its emphasis on team planning. Working together as a team builds organization-wide belief in and commitment to the plan, because it gives participants ownership in the plan and its projected results.

In many cases, it may appear that portions of this approach belabor the obvious. Yet how often has the "obvious" been the one thing you may have overlooked! For example, your company may be ready to move into a new market, only to discover that support materials specifically addressing that market have not been ordered. Or you may be installing a new inventory control system and you learn that no provision has been made for training related personnel. The planning process provides both a clear way to carry out the plan and a means for ensuring understanding and commitment to it. It is as necessary to the success of your organization as your people, financial resources, products, and technology. You cannot continue to succeed and grow without a clearly defined tactical plan.

Strategic planning focuses on the future direction and position of the organization. The first two books in this series focus, respectively, on strategic thinking and long-range planning, together covering the strategic aspects of planning. Tactical planning, the focus of this book, addresses implementation of the strategic plan and production of short-term results. Figure 2.2 provides an overview of the entire planning process. Note how each of the first two components of the process penetrates the next one, leading ultimately to effective plan implementation.

It is my observation that it is difficult, if not impossible, to do strategic and tactical planning at the same time. When you discuss both strategic and tactical issues, the urgency of your tactical concerns will tend to dominate. Strategic planning, on the one hand, is more intuitive than analytical and focuses largely on the external environment and factors that may require fundamental changes for an extended period. Tactical planning, on the other hand, is largely analytical, has more of an internal focus, and is much more specific and detailed.

Tactical planning plays a different role than strategic planning in your organization's planning process. Whereas the focus of strategic planning is on what your organization's business should be and what direction it should be moving in, tactical planning focuses on your organization's short-term destination and how it is going to get there. Tactical planning typically has a one-year horizon and is generally developed during the latter part of the prior fiscal year. Your

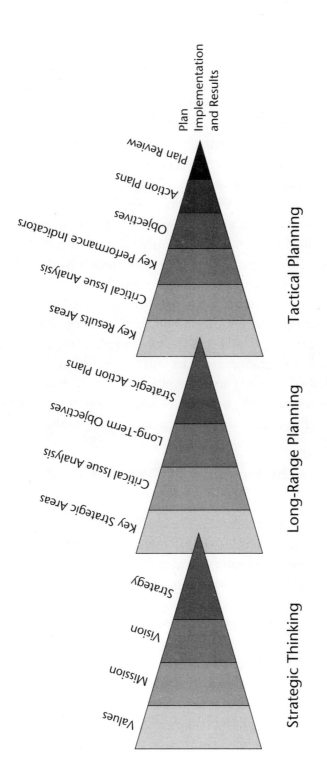

Figure 2.2 The Planning Process

Strategic Thinking

Values
Mission
Vision
Strategy

Long-Range Planning

Key Strategic Areas
Critical Issue Analysis
Long-Term Objectives
Strategic Action plans

Tactical Planning

Key Results Areas
Critical Issue Analysis
Key Performance Indicators
Objectives
Action Plans
Plan Review

Plan Implementation and Results

tactical plan needs to be developed *after* your strategic plan (which is usually prepared early in the year), since one purpose of your tactical plan is to implement a portion of your strategic plan.

The planning process may begin with either your strategic plan or your tactical plan, or some combination of both (developing a mission statement and then proceeding with a plan to achieve short-term results, for example), depending on your needs. It's important to note that the planning process is both nonlinear and iterative in nature. You may start with any *element* in the process that relates to your current need. Furthermore, the completion of certain elements may cause you to review assumptions and decisions made elsewhere in the plan, to ensure both consistency and accuracy of projections. As those who need to act in order to make your organization more successful become better informed about and more actively involved in the various planning steps, their commitment to significant results will become increasingly substantial. Remember, the purpose of planning is not primarily to produce plans; it is to produce results. Planning is a people process and the focus in this book is on making it work at all levels.

What Are the Elements of Tactical Planning and How Do They Fit Together?

The tactical planning process is made up of the six primary elements shown in Figure 2.3, which correspond to the elements of the tactical plan listed earlier. The process depicted in the figure is a slight adaptation of the MOR funnel that was first introduced in my various publications on management by objectives and results (see Annotated Resources). The emphasis in this book is more on organizational than on individual application.

The figure illustrates how managerial planning and decision making move from the broad and general to the narrow and specific. One way of making a plan more effective is to reduce the size of managerial decisions by breaking them into smaller pieces. We start with a relatively broad element, *Key Results Areas*, and get nar-

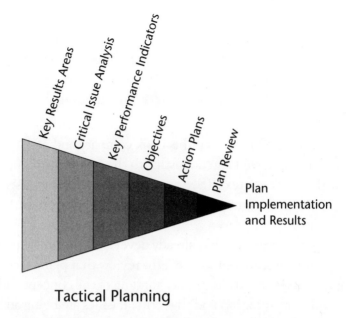

Tactical Planning

Figure 2.3 Elements of the Tactical Planning Process

rower and more specific as we move through the process. (For ease of communication, in the remainder of this book the words *plan* and *planning* should be interpreted as *tactical* unless otherwise indicated.)

You will notice that *Budgets* is not included in this planning model although it was a part of the model in one of my previous, coauthored books, *The Executive Guide to Operational Planning*. Is the preparation of organizational and unit budgets a part of the planning process? Of course! I have chosen *not* to include it here for three primary reasons:

1. Most organizations already have an established budgeting process and most managers must prepare their budgets in line with that process. Introducing a variation on that process, in my judgment, might tend to confuse middle and first-line managers who are using this book to guide their planning efforts.

2. For most managers preparation of budgets is an *event* while planning, as covered in this book, is an ongoing activity. By doing a systematic job of planning throughout the year, you will find it relatively easy to adapt your planning information to meet the requirements of your organization's budgeting process.

3. My intention is to keep this book compact and easy to follow. I do not believe I can do justice to the preparation of budgets within that context. (See the Annotated Resources section for some recommended books on budget preparation.)

If your organization has already developed a strategic plan, your first order of business, of course, is to review that plan. You want to be sure that there is a clear understanding of the concept and direction of the organization and that critical issues are being addressed. Your organization's statement of mission, in particular, is a critical foundation document to any planning effort. If there is no strategic plan to refer to, then you may wish to develop a statement of roles and missions for your organization or your unit as a first step in the process. (See the Appendix for instruction on developing a unit statement of roles and missions, which can also be adapted for use with the entire organization.)

Key Results Areas

These are the priority areas within which you need to achieve *results* during the projected planning period. The use of Key Results Areas ensures continuity in important performance areas that are essential to your organization's results. At the total organizational level, these are likely to include such areas as financial results, sales performance, customer service, and new product development. It may be helpful to look at some of your Key Results Areas in terms of their impact on important stakeholders such as owners/shareholders, customers, and employees. Normally, these areas will be broad enough to include results from more than one department or organizational segment. At the unit level (*unit* includes any distinct entity within the total organization, from a division or department to a one-person operation), Key Results Areas focus on the principal outputs of that particular unit, which could include such things as quality improvement, productivity, cost control, and employee morale.

Critical Issue Analysis

Here you will assess the current status of your organization's performance as well as the specific issues that will have substantial impact on your business during the coming year. It is at this point in the process that such factors as technological change, globalization, changing customer expectations, and other contemporary concerns need to be surfaced and analyzed. These issues may be in the form of assumptions that need to be reviewed and validated, as well as clearly identified issues. There are three primary sources of critical issues:

- Your organization's strategic plan, to help you identify factors requiring short-term attention—for example, the need for advertising materials to promote a new product or service that has been projected

- Your current year's plan and performance, for issues that will carry over into your next plan year—for example, increasing the number of people trained to perform a service for which there is increasing demand

- Other issues, current problems, or opportunities likely to impact your organization during the plan year—for example, a need to reduce costs to meet pressure from your competition

The analysis portion of this element is especially useful in helping you and those around you focus on identifying the *right* issues, validating them, and examining alternative ways of addressing them. Critical Issue Analysis is also valuable as an ongoing problem-solving and decision-making tool.

Key Performance Indicators

These are measurable factors within each of your Key Results Areas on which you may wish to set specific objectives. Since there are many ways in which your results can be measured, it's important that you clearly identify and agree on those indicators that will provide the *best visibility* on desired results. In addition, Key Performance Indicators frequently serve as factors you can track in monitoring progress toward the completion of your objectives. Some indicators are quantifiable, such as units or dollars of sales, units of production, and percentage of market share, and as such they are very useful and usually easy to track. Other indicators, however, that are not as easily quantified, such as program implementation, research and development capability, and new product introduction, are also valuable in assessing the type of results desired. In any case, the indicators selected must be understood and agreed to by those involved. (In previous books, I introduced the Indicator element immediately following Key Results Areas. My efforts with recent clients show a value in going through Critical Issue Analysis first as an additional means of identifying Key Performance Indicators.)

Objectives

These represent the specific, measurable results to be accomplished within the time span of your plan. They fall logically within one or more of your Key Results Areas and incorporate some of your Key Performance Indicators as their principal measurable factors. Objectives also may be developed in response to your Critical Issue Analysis. Objectives at the total organizational level normally require effort across unit lines and contain either a specific target date or an implied fiscal-year completion. They are limited to the major organizational accomplishments projected for the period of the plan. At the unit level, objectives tend to be narrower and more precise than at the organizational level. For example, your organization's objective to gain a 25 percent market share in a particular product line may require specific unit objectives by product and by region at lower levels. These objectives need to be either directly in support of the long-term objectives in your strategic plan (if one exists) or at least compatible with them. For specific results that are continuous in nature and may not require detailed action plans, such as minimum gross margin or monthly production quotas, the use of standards of performance, rather than objectives, may be more useful. As a variation on objectives, *standards of performance* are levels of achievement to be reached and then maintained on an ongoing basis.

Action Plans

These represent the specific actions required to accomplish each objective. They may be stated in one or a combination of the following three forms:

- Specific activities or events that are not necessarily interrelated
- A series of interconnected events following an analytical or problem-solving approach
- A series of smaller or shorter-term objectives

Your action plans will include specific time frames, resource requirements, and accountability for each step. They are also an effective way of validating (or invalidating) assumptions made in earlier steps.

Plan Review

Plan Review closes the loop in the planning process by ensuring that what you set out to accomplish actually gets translated into action that leads to results. This includes your asking three fundamental questions related to performance in the four basic elements of *time, resources, quality,* and *quantity*:

- What is likely to change?
- How and when will you know?
- What will you do?

Plan Review is designed to help you monitor performance against your objectives so that you can take corrective action or implement contingency plans when it becomes necessary.

How Do You Develop Your Tactical Plan?

Planning is a dynamic process that requires communication in all directions—top-down, bottom-up, and sideways—if it is to be effective. Clearly, there must be a sense of direction from the executive level of the organization for any kind of a cohesive plan to come together. There also needs to be input from the levels of the organization where the work gets done to make sure critical factors are not overlooked and that objectives being set have a reasonable likelihood of being achieved. Likewise, any plan that does not take into consideration both the support needed from and the impact on all related functions has little chance of being as successful as it could and should be.

One approach that seems to take advantage of the best aspects of these communication channels is what I refer to as the *Yo-Yo Approach*. Top management starts with a "fuzzy ball" that includes:

- A statement of direction that is consistent with the strategic plan
- A list of Key Results Areas for the total organization
- A list of "givens"—those results that are fixed and not subject to modification
- A list of critical issues, priorities, assumptions, and partially or fully completed analysis as appropriate

- A list of tentative objectives and suggested action plans
- Appropriate comments to guide managers throughout the organization in their decision making

This "fuzzy ball" is then rolled down the string and those managers with a vested interest have the opportunity to offer additions or modifications to the proposed plan based on perceived opportunities and needs. From that point, each manager will develop his or her own unit plan that includes what will be done to meet the unit's commitments to the total plan while carrying out its own roles and missions. This may require the "fuzzy ball" to be swung from side to side to ensure that appropriate coordination takes place between interfacing units. The "ball" is then rolled back up the string to see if its new shape is acceptable or whether additional modification may be required.

While this approach to planning requires more time than a strictly top-down approach, the potential payoff is well worth the investment of time and effort. A real sense of openness and flexibility on the part of both top management and unit leadership is necessary for this approach to work.

Two specific tools that will be especially useful as you assess where you are now with planning and prepare to implement the process are introduced in Chapter Nine. The *Planning Assessment Checklist* (see Figure 9.1) will help you identify what is going satisfactorily and where attention should be focused. The *Plan to Plan* (see Figure 9.3) will show you how to lay out a reasonable schedule for preparation of your plans.

What Are the Benefits of This Planning Process?

Planning, as described in this book, has several distinct benefits:

- It establishes a bridge to your organizations's strategic plan, ensuring compatibility of short-term results with long-term direction.

- It's an effective communication tool, linking your plans with those of others in your organization.
- It reduces the potential for semantic confusion by providing a common planning language throughout your organization.
- It can be adapted easily to address any unique planning or budgeting requirements you may have in your organization.
- It provides checks and balances to increase the probability that plans will address the real issues your organization is facing with specific results-oriented actions.
- It helps build teamwork throughout the organization, both within and between key organizational units.

In Summary

Tactical planning, the third component of the planning process,

- Is more analytical than intuitive
- Is the means for implementing your strategic plan
- Determines specific short-term results needed to carry out your organization's mission, vision, and strategy
- Produces practical documents that identify specific results to be achieved within a given period (usually one year), as well as the actions and resources required to achieve them
- Involves managers and key employees in producing tactical plans for their own units as well as for the total organization

The tactical planning process is made up of six primary elements:

1. Key Results Areas
2. Critical Issue Analysis
3. Key Performance Indicators

4. Objectives

5. Action Plans

6. Plan Review

The next six chapters will show you how to work with each of these elements.

CHAPTER THREE

What's Your Focus?

Determining Your Unit's Key Results Areas

Efficiency is doing things right; effectiveness is doing right things! This statement, attributed to Peter Drucker, emphasizes the importance of focusing on the *right* areas in which to invest time, energy, talent, and other resources in order to achieve results. Too many organizations work very hard to be efficient at things that may not need to be done at all. Key Results Areas (KRAs) will help you, as unit president, to concentrate your efforts in those performance categories that will produce the best results for you, your unit, and the organizations you serve.

What Are Key Results Areas?

Key Results Areas are just that: areas or categories of results that are essential to effective performance in your organization. Accomplishments within these areas are necessary if your organization is to carry out its mission successfully and meet the expectations generated through your plan. *Key Results Areas do not cover everything your unit will accomplish.* They identify broad headings under which your objectives are developed for approval and periodic review by your immediate supervisor and/or other higher-level body. They also provide a basis for identifying critical issues that may need to be analyzed before your objectives can be established.

As preparation for identifying critical issues and/or selecting objectives, the determination of your unit's KRAs is a vital element that helps you and your team isolate and categorize the kinds of results needed. You may find it helpful to identify KRAs that particularly impact certain stakeholders. Owners/shareholders will be interested in such things as revenue/sales, return/profit, and growth/diversification. Customers are affected by product quality, new products, and customer service. Employee development, productivity, and production planning will impact employees. Determining your KRAs also reduces the likelihood of overlooking factors that, while less visible than others, may nonetheless be vital to carrying out your unit's mission, such as cross-functional integration and customer/client/user relations. In addition, KRAs provide continuity in your plans from one year to the next by highlighting essential performance areas, such as public relations or safety, that may not be identified as current critical issues.

What Are Guidelines for Determining Your Key Results Areas?

The following basic guidelines can be used to help you determine your unit's KRAs. (A summary list is provided in Figure 3.1.)

Figure 3.1 Guidelines for Determining Your Key Results Areas

1. Identify those five to eight major areas within which your unit must achieve meaningful results during the coming year.
2. Identify both financial and nonfinancial areas.
3. Choose areas that directly or indirectly support your organization's strategic plan and other higher-level plans.
4. Don't expect your KRAs to cover your unit's entire output; instead, identify the vital few areas where priority efforts should be directed.
5. Realize that many KRAs will require cross-functional effort.
6. Each KRA should be limited generally to two or three words and should not be measurable as stated but should contain factors that could be made measurable.

---

1.   *Identify those five to eight major areas within which your unit must achieve meaningful results during the coming year.* Certain KRAs, such as operating results and productivity, may be ongoing and included in every plan. Others, such as product/service development or organizational image, may be included only when they are identified as critical issues.

2.   *Include both financial and nonfinancial areas.* While bottom-line results are always of concern, they do not, and should not, represent the total picture of your organization's performance. Such things as product/service quality, research and development, and employee development represent an equally important part of the total picture.

3.   *Choose areas that directly or indirectly support your organization's strategic plan and other higher-level plans.* Your KRAs should be able to be linked with one or more elements of your strategic plan and other related organizational plans.

4.   *Don't expect your KRAs to cover your unit's entire output; instead, identify the vital few areas where priority efforts should be directed.* Many things that will be accomplished within your unit are essential for its ongoing performance but will not be of critical concern to others. This is part of the reason for limiting the number of KRAs to five to eight. That limitation forces you and your planning team to determine which are the few truly vital areas where your attention needs to be addressed.

5.   *Realize that many KRAs will require cross-functional effort.* At the total organization level, most KRAs will require the active participation of two or more major functions or organizational segments. Some areas, such as product quality or customer service, may require the active involvement of the entire organization. KRAs for your unit should also take into consideration your interdependence with other units, perhaps identified as internal customer relations or cross-functional integration.

6.   *Each KRA should be limited generally to two or three words and should not be measurable as stated but should contain factors that could*

be made measurable. KRAs should be specific enough to identify the kinds of results you need but general enough to provide flexibility and, as appropriate, more than one specific result. Limiting your KRAs to short phrases makes it easier to focus on the specific results needed.

Figure 3.2 contains several examples of KRAs appropriate to many organizations, and Figure 3.3 shows KRAs that are frequently used within specific organizational units. These should not be seen as prescriptive lists, however. Some of these areas will not apply to you, and undoubtedly there are several other areas appropriate to your organization or unit that do not appear here. The KRAs you select should be stated in terms that are relevant to you and others who must relate to them.

Figure 3.2 Examples of Organizational Key Results Areas

Revenue/sales	Product/service line performance
Return/profit	Product/service quality
Growth/diversification	New product/service development
Acquisitions	Research and development
New market development	Employee development
Customer satisfaction	Organizational image
Customer service	Public relations
Operating results	Safety

Figure 3.3 Examples of Unit Key Results Areas

Unit production/output	Product/service design
Cost control/management	Program/project management
Quality control/assurance	Production planning
Productivity	Unit administration
Customer/client/user relations	Vendor/supplier relations
Employee development/relations	Cross-functional integration

In Summary

- KRAs provide your first planning breakdown of performance areas where you need to focus your organization's or unit's primary efforts.
- They will not cover everything your unit will accomplish.
- They will help segment your total performance so you can determine the results for which you will be held accountable.
- They include both normal work output, which may be going satisfactorily, and critical issues where special attention is required.

The next chapter will help you identify and analyze critical issues that will have a major impact on your unit's performance during the current or projected plan year.

What's Important?

Identifying and Analyzing Your Critical Issues

Critical issue analysis is a powerful planning tool that is as useful in problem or opportunity situations as it is in the regular planning process. It provides a discipline to offset the natural tendency of many managers to move immediately from a perceived issue or problem to a solution. While I do not discount the value of managerial intuition (which is a particularly vital part of the strategic planning process), we frequently don't have enough information to make the most appropriate decisions in most tactical situations. Furthermore, completing a critical issue analysis frequently helps us redefine the issue in a way that increases the probability that we will be setting our objectives on the *right* things. This is why objectives are not set until *after* we have determined our key results areas, analyzed our critical issues, and identified our key performance indicators. Key results areas help us focus our attention on where results are needed. Critical issue analysis helps us identify and resolve our most important issues.

What Is Critical Issue Analysis?

Critical issue analysis begins with your assessment of your unit's performance and the major issues that need to be addressed during the period of your tactical plan. It also provides a key link between your strategic and tactical plans. It helps you take a look at the impact of your assumptions about what is happening in the world, as well as at your capabilities and resources. Critical issue analysis leads you and your planning team to specific conclusions and alternative courses of action on the most important issues affecting your unit's performance.

You could easily identify twenty or thirty issues that need attention. However, there is no way you can deal effectively with that many concerns. Critical issue analysis provides a basis for selection of the vital few issues (typically four to eight) that will impact your unit's results the most. It also

- Builds an information base from which you can develop realistic objectives and action plans
- Helps validate or invalidate your business assumptions
- Helps avoid premature decisions
- Maintains focus on the vital few issues
- Helps identify key performance indicators that otherwise might be overlooked
- Makes certain that both long-term and short-term needs are being met
- Helps reduce or eliminate the expenditure of resources (human and material) on low-value issues
- Provides an excellent vehicle for team decision making and fixing accountability for action

What Is Involved in Critical Issue Analysis?

There are four primary steps in Critical Issue Analysis:

1. *Identifying issues.* The first and most obvious step is to identify your *perceived* issues, which could represent either problems or opportunities. It's important to recognize that these issues are considered only as perceived until they have been validated through the analysis process. Your KRAs will help you identify many potential issues. Issues also may be drawn from any or all of the following sources:

- Your strategic plan (conceptual and long-term)
- Your current tactical plan (specific and short-term)
- Actual performance (including current opportunities or problems)

Figure 4.1 contains examples of critical issues gleaned from these sources.

Figure 4.1 Examples of Critical Issues for the Total Organization

Source	Critical Issues
Strategic plan	• Need for new product focus • Inadequate manufacturing capability
Current tactical plan	• Shrinking customer base • Declining margins • Need for additional customer service capability
Performance problems and/or opportunities	• Poor delivery performance • Major competitor with serious quality problems

---

The same process may be applied to identifying critical issues at the unit level. However, unit issues will generally be more specific and directly related to your unit's roles and missions. Also, some of the issues you need to address in your unit may be referred to you from higher-level management as a part of their critical issue analysis. Figure 4.2 shows how some of the critical issues for the total organization might be identified at the unit level.

When a relatively large number of issues are identified, it may be useful to group them under their related KRAs in order to reduce overlap and to aid in the prioritization step.

2. *Prioritizing issues.* Determine the four to eight most important perceived issues—those that are likely to have the greatest impact. Choosing a limited number that truly represent the vital few issues ensures that they are likely to receive the attention they deserve. Other identified issues need to be disposed of in some way,

Figure 4.2 Examples of Critical Issues at the Unit Level

Organizational Issue	Potential Unit Issues
Need for new product focus	Sales: new product sales incentives Marketing: greater predictability of market trends R&D: targeted new product development Manufacturing: retooling requirements
Declining margins	Sales: excessive sales expense Marketing: improper pricing Purchasing: excessive raw material costs Manufacturing: excessive production costs
Poor delivery performance	Sales: unrealistic delivery commitments Distribution: excessive turnaround time Manufacturing: delays in production flow

such as by referring them to specific departments, work units, or individuals, combining them with related issues on the list, retaining them for later consideration, or eliminating them.

3.   *Analyzing issues.* This is the most crucial step in the analysis process. It involves both validating a particular issue and developing effective ways for addressing it.

4.   *Summarizing issues.* The specific conclusions and alternative courses of action need to be summarized in a way that will make it easy to prepare your objectives and action plans.

These steps are discussed in greater detail in the next section.

How Do You Complete a Critical Issue Analysis?

Identifying Issues

There are several effective techniques for identifying issues:

1. You may ask the members of your planning team to complete a questionnaire either in advance of or during the first part of

the initial planning meeting. Individual responses to these questions may be shared and consolidated into a list of unit issues, including both problems and opportunities. Develop your own list of questions such as:

What are the four to eight most critical issues facing our unit in the coming year? What impact will each of these issues have on our performance?

What issues are likely to have the greatest effect on profitability (or short-term results)?

What issues are likely to make the greatest contribution to long-term success?

What changes have taken place or are likely to take place during the coming year that will significantly affect our unit's performance?

What problems or opportunities within our unit or between us and other units are likely to impact our performance?

What resource limitations or opportunities need to be addressed?

2. You may wish to use brainstorming to identify potential issues. Many issues are readily apparent to your team members, who just need an open forum and the time to bring them out. Your unit's KRAs will help provide focus during this process. This technique can also be used to supplement responses to your questionnaire.

3. Existing strategic and tactical plans, including your unit's performance to these plans, should be reviewed to identify any additional factors that need to be added to your issues list.

4. Assumptions made about markets, product acceptance, competition, and other external factors should be examined to determine their current validity.

5. Current performance reports from individuals within or outside your unit may identify some issues that otherwise might be overlooked.

6. Publications related to your industry or markets may reveal several other factors that need to be considered as you develop your issues list.

Your next step is to review all of the potential issues on your list and eliminate or combine those that are duplications as well as reword those that may be confusing. Some of your issues that address factors external to your organization will be more useful if stated in terms you can deal with effectively. For example, "uncertain market economy" could be stated as "need for contingency plans to meet fluctuations in the economy."

Since you may end up with twenty or thirty or more potential issues, you may find it useful to group them under their respective KRAs before attempting to prioritize them. In that way, you may more easily identify duplications, as well as focus on related issues at the same time. You will find it easier to go through the prioritization process if your list is limited to no more than ten to fifteen potential issues.

Prioritizing Issues

Having clarified and modified the potential issues and reduced them to a manageable number, your team should next agree on the four to eight most important issues for your unit to address during the coming year. A simple, but effective, technique for prioritizing is as follows:

1. Have each individual team member evaluate each of the remaining issues using a 3-2-1 weighting factor, with 3 being both important and urgent, 2 being important but not urgent, and 1 representing issues that could be deferred or that you may not have the ability or resources to address. You may wish to limit the number of issues in each category (such as one third of the total).

2. On a chart, record the weighting factors identified by each individual team member alongside each issue.

3. Compile priorities based on both the number of responses and the weighted average.

4. Discuss the issues to ensure team agreement on priorities.

As stated earlier, issues not included in the final list may be referred to specific departments, work units, or individuals for resolution, combined with related issues on the list, retained for later consideration, or simply dropped.

Analyzing Issues

Once you have reached agreement on the most important issues, the next action is to validate each issue as legitimate and develop alternative ways for addressing each issue. Two effective methods for this step are *group discussion* and *individual assignments* to be presented at a subsequent meeting. For each priority issue, there must be team consensus on responses to the following questions:

- What is the issue?
- What data/information is available (or needed) to either validate or invalidate this issue? (It's important to focus strictly on data, not opinion, here. What tangible evidence is there to justify putting time and effort into resolving this issue?)
- What appear to be the factors causing this to be an issue for the organization? (Opinions may be included here, preferably backed up by verifiable data.)
- What types of results are needed in this area? (These may be counterbalancing to some of the causes or they may focus on more encompassing results.)

Summarizing Issues

Once you and your team have identified, prioritized, and analyzed the issues, you need to summarize them into conclusions and alternative courses of action to be considered. The following questions need to be addressed here:

- What conclusions can be drawn from this analysis that will provide direction for specific action?

- What are alternative ways of acting on these conclusions? (Identify as many alternatives as possible to provide some reasonable choices.)

The answers to these questions will form the basis for identifying key performance indicators, setting objectives, and preparing action plans to address the issues.

What Are Some Examples of Critical Issue Analysis?

Figure 4.3 provides an example of a completed critical issue analysis using all four steps that was adapted from the plan of a medium-size manufacturing company. Some of the details from the actual plan have been deleted to simplify the illustration. The critical issues shown under the first step came as a result of consolidating the issues identified in a brainstorming session.

Figure 4.4 is a conceptual worksheet for taking a critical issue through the analysis process from issue identification through objectives and action steps. (Critical issue analysis ends after the identification of Alternative Courses of Action. The remaining process elements are covered in subsequent chapters; they are included in the figure to show the linkage among all elements.) Figure 4.5 is an example of a completed worksheet addressing the issue of lack of sufficient customer orientation throughout a company. Figure 4.6 is an example of a critical issue related to the lack of depth of personnel at the department level.

In Summary

Critical issue analysis is the second step in the development of your plan, following determination of key results areas.

- It ensures integration with existing strategic and tactical plans by identifying, prioritizing, analyzing, and summarizing critical tactical issues.

- It keeps you from jumping too quickly toward a solution before the issue is clearly understood.

- It enables your planning team to agree on key conclusions for resolving the most important issues.

- It leads to important inputs for other organizational unit plans.

The next chapter will show you how to measure your results through the use of Key Performance Indicators.

Figure 4.3   Sample Critical Issue Analysis

---

1. *Identify issues.*

Source	Perceived Issues
Strategic plan	• Current markets insufficient to meet growth goals
	• Technological obsolescence of some current products
	• Marketing efforts not responsive to customers' technological needs
	• Need to balance long-term growth and profitability
	• Insufficient sales and engineering personnel to support future product and market requirements
	• Lack of sufficient customer orientation throughout the company
Current tactical plan	• Insufficient information on customers' future requirements
	• Lack of technological focus in R&D programs
	• Overdependence on parts sales to meet profit requirements
	• Facility lease renewal
	• Declining backlog
Current performance problems/opportunities	• Insufficient technical support to sales
	• Need for new machining supplier
	• Increasing material costs
	• Loss of market share to competitor X
	• Competition not addressing customers' *future* requirements (opportunity)

2. *Prioritize issues.*   (The following issues, with further clarification, were adopted by the executive team as having the greatest impact on the company during the coming year. Remaining issues were either delegated to specific departments for action, incorporated into the following issues, or tabled for later review by the executive team.)

• Current markets insufficient to meet growth goals
• Technological obsolescence of some current products
• Lack of technological focus in R&D programs
• Insufficient technical support to sales
• Overdependence on parts sales to meet profit requirements

Figure 4.3 Sample Critical Issue Analysis, Cont'd.

---

3. *Analyze issues.* (Following is one issue that was analyzed by members of the executive team. The other prioritized issues received similar treatment.)

Perceived Issue:
- Technological obsolescence of some current products (specified)

Data/information:
- Competitor X's products provide additional features (specified).
- Customers A & B have asked us to match competitor X's features or they will switch.
- Our (specified) products were introduced four years ago and achieved a 40 percent market share by end of first year.
- Our market share for these products has been declining for the past eighteen months and is currently 28 percent.

Probable Causes:
- R&D focus has been on new products, not on improving existing products.
- Current manufacturing processes cannot accommodate features similar to those provided by competitor X.
- We have been unwilling to invest capital needed.
- Competitor X is aggressively pursuing our customer base.

Results needed:
- Redesigned (specified) products must include same features as provided by competitor X, plus additional improvements.
- Upgraded products must be available within six months.
- Cost of products must remain competitive.
- New capital is required to complete necessary retooling.

4. *Summarize issues.* (Using the information provided as a result of data analysis, the executive team agreed on the following conclusions and alternative courses of action.)

Conclusions:
- Top priority will be given by R&D to redesign of these products, with a targeted completion of sixty days, which may require the delay of some current projects.
- Manufacturing must prepare for transition to upgraded products, including necessary retooling, to minimize downtime.
- Sales will negotiate with current customers to agree to use current products until upgraded products are available.

Figure 4.3 Sample Critical Issue Analysis, Cont'd.

Alternative courses of action:

R&D
- Dedicate (specified) engineers to work on project full time.
- Retain outside firm to complete redesign under supervision of (specified) project engineer.

Manufacturing
- Purchase existing plant to convert to upgraded products.
- Contract with subcontractor to provide manufacturing capability.
- Consolidate existing product manufacturing into Building A and add a shift to meet current demands; Building B to be dedicated to upgraded products.

Sales
- Offer price incentives to customers to continue with current products until upgraded products are available.
- Provide priority delivery of upgraded products to current customers in return for temporary continued use of current products.
- Offer price concessions on upgraded products in return for temporary continued use of current products.

Figure 4.4 Worksheet for Analyzing a Critical Issue

Critical Issue Analysis and Plan

Key Results Area:

Perceived Issue:

Data/Information (facts, not opinions):

Probable Causes (both facts and opinions acceptable):

Results Needed:

Conclusion(s):

Alternative Courses of Action:

Key Performance Indicators:

Objective(s):

Others Impacted:

Action Steps:

Figure 4.5 Example of Critical Issue Development

Key Results Area: Customer Relations

Perceived Issue: Lack of sufficient customer orientation throughout the company

Data/Information (facts, not opinions):
- Identification of each department's customers (internal and external)
- Specific data from past when customers were *not* the primary focus
- Recorded customer complaints
- Identification of areas in which increased attention to customer needs is warranted

Probable Causes (both facts and opinions acceptable):
- Historic emphasis on production, safety, and so on, rather than on customer concerns
- Historic perception that customers are only external, not internal to the organization
- Insufficient training in customer service
- No clear perception of who our "customers" really are or why it is important to treat them as customers

Results Needed:
- Employees will be educated about the need for customers, what a customer is, and why they are important.
- Each department will identify its customers.
- Key performance indicators of customer satisfaction will be defined and made measurable.
- Each department will review its customer service indicators and performance and set specific goals for improving customer satisfaction/service.

Conclusion(s): We will provide customer service training and establish clear, measurable goals related to improving customer satisfaction/service for the company as a whole and for each department. This may require the realignment of some managerial and employee responsibilities.

Alternative Courses of Action:
- Formal training in customer service by company staff or outside training organization
- Informal meetings with employees on a regular basis related to customer concerns
- Informal meetings between departments and their identified customers
- Survey of customers to establish a customer service index from which improvement goals can be set
- Regular reports on progress toward achieving customer-related goals

---

Figure 4.5 Example of Critical Issue Development, Cont'd.

(The following show how the analysis was converted into specific plans.)

Key Performance Indicators:
- Percentage increase in customer service index (based on survey results)
- Frequency of department/customer group meetings with mutually agreed-upon objectives

Objective: To complete a minimum of one department/customer group meeting for each department each quarter, with mutually agreed-upon objectives, at an average per-meeting cost not to exceed $100 and thirty work-hours

Others Impacted: Staff support groups, customer groups, department heads.

Action Steps:
1. Get agreement/commitment from department heads and related staff groups.
2. Have each department identify its customers and reach agreement on a plan.
3. Develop and schedule training sessions for department heads and facilitators.
4. Follow up on progress and modify plans as needed.

Figure 4.6 Example of a Departmental Critical Issue Analysis

Key Results Area: Departmental Performance

Perceived Issue: Insufficient depth in key department functions

Data/Information (facts, not opinions):
- Schedule delays (be specific)
- Rework required
- Work stoppage when key person absent

Probable Causes (both facts and opinions acceptable):
- Rapid promotions
- Overdependence on key individuals
- Insufficient training in key skills
- Current workload requirements

Results Needed:
- Key employees need to be trained to perform additional functions.
- Greater depth is required in people qualified to perform key functions.

Conclusion(s): We will provide ongoing development opportunities for key people to ensure sufficient depth in key functions and to be prepared to meet future challenges. This will require planned slippages in some current projects to permit time for training.

(This is also an example of converting analysis into specific plans.)

Alternative Courses of Action:
- Formal training, informal cross-training
- Hire additional people
- Realign project schedule
- Say "no" to projects we cannot handle

Key Performance Indicators:
- Number of direct reports with implemented development plans
- Number of backups for key positions
- Number qualified for promotion

Objective: To have a minimum of two qualified backups for each key position by September 30 at a cost not to exceed $10,000 and three hundred work-hours

Others Impacted: Department managers, key individuals, selected user departments, corporate training department

Action Steps:
1. Identify and agree on "key positions."
2. Determine knowledge and skill required.
3. Identify and get commitment of people to be trained.
4. Identify and prioritize projects and reach agreement with users on new schedules.
5. Determine and implement required training/development plans.
6. Review progress weekly.
7. Follow up.

CHAPTER FIVE

How Should You Measure Your Results?

Selecting Your Key Performance Indicators

If you are like many managers I have met, a major challenge you have in the planning process is to figure out how to measure what you intend to accomplish. Generally, it is not difficult to describe what you and others within your unit do and, perhaps, the amount of time you spend doing it. However, describing what you do in terms of accomplishments is much more difficult. This is especially true in service or support organizations, which may not have hard numbers such as sales volume or products shipped by which to measure their results.

If this kind of measurement has been a problem for you, you may find Key Performance Indicators (KPIs) to be one of the most useful tools available. The key word here is *indicators*—nothing more, nothing less. Measurability is a relative matter, of course, since nothing is absolute. While indicators are measurable, *there are no absolute measures in the planning process; indicators only suggest the probability of worthwhile results*. And KPIs are not limited to numbers, as we shall see later. The important consideration is that you will be focusing on the *results* you intend to produce, not on the *effort* required to produce them.

What Are Key Performance Indicators?

Key Performance Indicators are those measurable factors within a given Key Results Area (KRA) on which it may be worthwhile to set objectives. They generally describe *what* will be measured, not how much or by when (those come in the objectives). Their primary purpose is to identify the kind of measurable outputs desired in each of your KRAs. They provide the tangibility that is needed to lend substance to each of these areas. Properly selected KPIs also provide you with the most relevant information for tracking the desired results.

KPIs have at least four uses in the planning process:

1. Identifying a list of potential measurable factors in each KRA
2. Selecting those measurable factors on which objectives should be set at this time
3. Establishing specific action steps for accomplishing those objectives
4. Tracking performance related to objectives and action plans

Of these uses, the most important is the second one, which helps you define the specific targets in each of your objectives.

One of the exciting things that happens in the process of identifying KPIs is the mind stretching that takes place through dialogue among members of your planning team. While for some KRAs the specific outcomes or objectives are so obvious you can move immediately into setting your objectives, in most areas there is a real benefit in exploring the wide variety of KPIs that might be used. If you and your planning team go through the process of identifying as many potential indicators as might be appropriate to a given KRA, there is a much greater likelihood that the *right* results will be identified when you select your objectives. These results may or may not be the ones that have been used previously or that appear most obvious at the outset.

An additional value from identifying several KPIs for each KRA is that you can help pinpoint other factors that would be useful to track as part of your control or feedback system even if they are not included in your objectives. This is an important consideration in planning a closed-loop system. Certain KPIs that may not be applicable to your current plan may be useful in future planning efforts.

What Are Guidelines for Identifying Your KPIs?

Under normal circumstances, KPIs should meet the following criteria (a summary of these criteria is provided in Figure 5.1):

1. *They should be measurable factors, falling logically within a given KRA, on which objectives may be set.* There are many factors, such as cash flow, quality standards, and delivery schedules, that may prove very useful for tracking performance at the total organizational level but that may not be especially helpful in defining your objectives.

2. *They may be selected from any or all of the following types:*

- *Hard numbers*, such as sales, units of production, products shipped, and clients served
- *Percentages*, such as profit margins, market share, sales to new customers, repeat business, and productivity increases
- *Significant achievements*, such as major project completions (or milestones), certifications, new service capability, and performance awards
- *Service factors*, such as response time, frequency of contact, and customer acceptance

---

Figure 5.1 Guidelines for Identifying Key Performance Indicators

---

1. They should be measurable factors, falling logically within a given Key Results Area, on which objectives may be set.
2. They may be selected from any or all of the following types:
   - Hard numbers
   - Percentages
   - Significant achievements
   - Service factors
   - Problems to be overcome
   - Soft or indirect indicators
3. They should identify what will be measured, not how much or in what direction.
4. They should represent factors that can be tracked on an ongoing basis to the extent possible.
5. The cost of identifying and monitoring them should not exceed the value of the information obtained.

- *Problems to be overcome,* such as excess inventory, schedule slippages, quality deficiencies, and cost overruns

- *Soft or indirect indicators,* which may suggest effectiveness in subjective areas such as turnover or absenteeism (related to employee morale) and survey results (related to customer service)

3. *They should identify what will be measured, not how much or in what direction.* Focusing specifically on the *factor* to be measured usually provides for greater objectivity in making sure you have selected the most appropriate KPI. Identifying the specific numbers or results desired before you have considered other alternatives might lead to premature selection of the KPI (and the objective) because of its emotional appeal. For example, a KPI identified as "10 percent increase in market share" (which is almost an objective) might look very attractive. Prematurely selecting that as the indicator, however, could result in your overlooking the impact it would have on developing new products, which might not produce short-term results but could have tremendous future potential. A KPI such as "new products introduced" together with one on "percent market share" might provide a more balanced perspective from which realistic objectives could be established.

4. *They should represent factors that can be tracked on an ongoing basis to the extent possible.* KPIs that can only be measured after they have been completed, such as acquisitions, are acceptable in certain areas. However, when KPIs can be identified in such a way that they can be tracked as ongoing trends, such as sales growth or percentage of repeat business, they are much more useful as a part of the total planning process.

5. *The cost of identifying and monitoring KPIs should not exceed the value of the information.* This is a judgment call. For example, measuring the level of individual performance using a piece of equipment or software might provide valuable insight in terms of the reliability of that equipment or software. However, the cost of obtaining that information is likely to be prohibitive. A representative sampling would probably be nearly as useful at a much lower cost.

Figure 5.2 contains examples of KPIs for selected KRAs.

Figure 5.2 Examples of Key Performance Indicators

Key Results Areas	Key Performance Indicators
Return/profit	Return on investment Percentage of return on sales Net profit before taxes (dollars) Percentage of gross margin (by product line)
Productivity	Dollars of sales per employee Units per month (by product line) Output per work-hour Output per employee Overtime as percentage of payroll Downtime Turnaround time
Employee development	Training investment as percentage of sales Number of employees on degree plan Cross-training plan Number of backups per position Number of employees with implemented development plan
Quality assurance	Percentage of first-time acceptance Yield Cost of rework, scrap Percentage of error-free completions (per shift, per employee) Percentage of recidivism (in law enforcement)
Cross-functional integration	Percentage of on-time completions Number of unresolved conflicts Average lead time on support requests Specific joint project agreements
Research and development	Number of new product ideas approved for development Projected dollar value of approved product ideas Number of new applications for current products/services Cost of R&D investment: ratio to total budget
Organizational image	Favorable mentions in media Public information programs Involvement in community Interorganizational cooperative efforts
Legislative relations	Response time to legislators Inquiries handled favorably Funding approved Major programs approved

In Summary

Key Performance Indicators are those measurable factors that will help you

- Identify the specific results to be achieved within each Key Results Area
- Address critical issues you have identified and validated
- Establish specific action steps
- Track performance

Remember, the primary purpose of identifying Key Results Areas and Key Performance Indicators is to enable you to establish the *right* Objectives at the *right* time. This process will be addressed in the next chapter.

CHAPTER SIX

What Are Your Targets?

Establishing Your Objectives and Standards

A frequently heard statement in the retail industry is that the three most important things to consider are location, location, and location. A board member of a client organization paraphrased that statement by saying that the three most important things in a profitable company are objectives, objectives, and objectives. While this is a bit of an oversimplification, there is no doubt that the selection and formulation of objectives is the focal point of any plan. This is the first time in the process when you can focus on the specific *results* your unit needs to accomplish. The purpose of the first three elements of your plan—key results areas, critical issue analysis, and key performance indicators—is primarily to help determine what objectives should be selected. The next element—action plans—identifies *how* you will achieve them.

What Are Objectives and Where Do They Come From?

Objectives are statements of measurable results to be accomplished within the time frame of your plan (usually one year). At the total organizational level, these objectives normally will be limited to the most important accomplishments projected for that period, and typically they represent effort that crosses organizational lines. They carry either specific target dates or an implied fiscal-year completion. They include but are not limited to projected financial results. They represent targets at which the entire organization will be shooting as the plan progresses. As unit president, you of course must focus on the specific objectives your "company" must achieve to carry out your mission and meet your commitments to the larger organization.

Your primary sources of objectives are the conclusions reached and alternative courses of action identified during your critical issue analysis, as well as the determination of your KRAs and KPIs. Other major sources are the long-term objectives and strategic action plans included in your organization's strategic plan or other high-level plans, if they have not already been reviewed during your critical issue analysis. Additional sources are the personal convictions of the CEO and other key people in your organization. Also, the members of the board of directors, who represent the interests of the owners and are usually charged with approval or rejection of the total organization's plan, may provide input to the selection of objectives. If your organization is part of a larger body, such as a parent company or superagency, they may have specific requirements that you need to consider as well.

How Many Objectives Should You Have and Where Do Standards Fit In?

One of the purposes of establishing objectives is to highlight those projected accomplishments that you, your team, and your immediate supervisor should be reviewing on a regular basis. For most organizational units, six to ten objectives with written action plans is an appropriate number. In addition, there may be several standards of performance, frequently related to financial and operating results, that will be tracked on a regular basis. A standard of performance represents a level of achievement to be reached and then maintained on an ongoing basis, which therefore needs to be monitored but may not require a written action plan. Figure 6.1 provides some examples of such standards.

It's neither desirable nor practical to write objectives on everything that should be accomplished during the period of your plan.

Figure 6.1 Examples of Standards of Performance

Key Results Areas	Standards of Performance
Profit	Minimum gross margin of 35 percent
Unit output	1,000 units per shift
Product quality	Maximum three rejects per 1,000 units
Safety	No lost-time accidents
Productivity	Maximum turnaround of twenty-four hours on shipments

---

That would simply be unmanageable. Many things are accomplished whether or not objectives are set regarding them. Written objectives should highlight those things of such vital importance that continual focus on them is required. The greater the number of objectives projected, the less likely it is that each will receive the attention that is necessary. In addition, the paperwork generated by a large number of objectives could prove overwhelming. Objectives that are regularly reviewed at the executive level should represent those things that will have a major impact on moving the organization in the direction in which it must go. Furthermore, objectives at this level need to be of vital concern to all members of the executive team, not just to one or two team members. The same principle applies at the unit level, although most of these objectives will be much narrower and more specific than those at the total organizational level.

How Do You Select Your Objectives?

The process for selecting objectives at the total organizational level usually takes place in a planning meeting. A coach/facilitator may guide the team through agreement on KRAs and KPIs that clearly need to be considered, as well as on conclusions and alternative courses of action for addressing critical issues. For each KRA, one or more objectives should be identified. These may be constructed by the total planning team during the meeting itself, or individuals or subgroups within the planning team may develop proposed objectives for presentation to the entire group. In either case, objectives being considered need to be discussed at length to make certain that all pertinent factors have been examined and that the team is in agreement with what is being proposed. At this stage, it may be appropriate to identify a relatively long list of objectives as an initial effort, with the expectation that they will be reviewed a second and possibly a third time to determine which are the primary objectives that need to be included in the projected plan with written action plans. Remaining objectives on this list can be incorporated into some of the other objectives, assigned to individual members of the team for implementation at a lower level, or retained for later review and possible implementation. For example, an objective related to reducing lost-time accidents probably should be handled by the production department, with periodic reports given to the executive team if the objective is a major concern.

Within your unit, you may wish to follow a similar process, using a coach/facilitator; or you may opt for a more informal setting with your team. In some cases, it may make sense to develop your objectives by yourself and then review them with others who will be involved or impacted by them. You will need to set aside some uninterrupted time when you will be able to concentrate on developing the objectives that will produce the best overall results for you, your unit, and your total organization.

What Are Guidelines for Writing Your Objectives?

The following discussion of guidelines for well-stated objectives will aid you in the formulation of your objectives. Although a given objective will not necessarily conform to all of these criteria, it should nonetheless be checked against each of them. Only when you have made a conscious determination that a specific criterion does not apply should it be bypassed as a factor in validating a particular objective.

1.   *An objective should start with the word "to" followed by an action or accomplishment verb.* Since an objective is a statement of results, there is action involved. However, that action should clearly reflect the achievement of something, not merely the carrying out of an activity. It's important that the statement of your objective not reinforce *activity* as an end in itself. While activity will be required to accomplish your objective, that activity is more appropriately addressed in the action plan. Thus, the verb you select should focus on the *result*, not the activity. For example, verbs such as *complete, acquire,* and *produce* suggest accomplishment, whereas verbs such as *develop, conduct,* and *disseminate* imply activity.

2.   *An objective should specify a single measurable result to be accomplished.* What is the one key measurement that will tell whether or not an objective has been achieved? Your KPIs will be especially helpful in determining what that measurement should be. Most objectives will produce a wide variety of results. It's important to select one key measurement that provides an overriding indication of your desired results. For example, in evaluating market penetration you need to determine whether total dollar sales in a particular market or percentage of market share is the critical KPI. Either measure could provide the result desired, but placing both measures into the objective could prove cumbersome and, in some cases, the two could prove to be incompatible (since the database to be measured is different with each indicator). In cases where it may be appropriate to identify several different but related results, as with the above example, having more than one objective may be the solution.

3.   *An objective should specify a target date or time span for completion.* This is an essential factor to ensure timely action. Even though some objectives have an implied plan-year completion, specific deadlines, either for the total objective or for interim steps, need to be discussed thoroughly and included in the action plan if

not in the objective itself. Certain objectives (particularly those that are project oriented) for which completion is anticipated before or after the end of the plan period need to have the target date included in the objective itself. At the unit level, identifying specific target dates usually becomes especially important.

4.   *An objective should specify maximum cost factors*. Before you commit to any objective, you need to have an understanding of the resources required, even though you may not know the precise amount until you develop your action plan. These resources include time and effort required as well as out-of-pocket costs. The value of any objective is in direct proportion to the cost of achieving it. Identifying costs associated with an objective gives you an opportunity to validate it when you develop your action plan. Furthermore, it provides a more rational basis for making trade-off decisions in determining which objectives should be pursued and which ones should be placed on hold. While identifying costs on some organizational objectives, such as those in the financial area, may not be feasible, it's important to establish some limitations on objectives related to programs, such as new products or information systems development, as guidance for implementation as well as control. You may therefore consider it *optional* whether or not to include the cost factor in the objective itself, particularly at the top level of the organization. The inclusion of cost limitations becomes much more practical and necessary at lower-unit levels, where such costs are more readily identifiable. Regardless of whether or not cost is included in the objective, an examination of estimated costs is a critical consideration in determining the value of any objective.

These first four guidelines are primarily concerned with the construction of an objective. A model for a well-stated objective is shown in Figure 6.2, together with four typical examples. The remaining four guidelines provide additional aid in the effective preparation of your unit's objectives.

5.   *An objective should be as specific and quantitative (and hence measurable and verifiable) as possible*. The objective "to increase sales to existing customers" has little meaning. The objective "to increase sales to existing customers by a minimum of 10 percent" provides

---

Figure 6.2 Model and Examples of Well-Stated Objectives

Model:

To (action/accomplishment verb)   (single measurable result)
by (target date/time span)   *at* (cost in time and/or money)

Examples:

- To complete the Acme project by December 31 at a cost not to exceed $50,000 and five hundred work-hours.
- To decrease the average cost of sales by a minimum of 5 percent, effective June 1, at an implementation cost not to exceed forty work-hours.
- To release product A to manufacturing by September 30 at a cost not to exceed $50,000 and five thousand engineering hours.
- To reduce average turnaround time on service requests from eight to six hours by July 31 at an implementation cost of forty work-hours.

---

something specific to shoot for. The specific target, of course, will have been assessed during critical issue analysis. Although many types of objectives lend themselves easily to quantification through the use of numbers or percentages, just as many do not. This is where the KPI element is especially useful. The completion, addition, or elimination of something is just as measurable as a set of numbers. An example would be "to complete installation of a fully automated production line by (date)." The key is in reaching agreement among the members of the planning team on what specific measurable factors will be used.

6. *An objective should specify only the* what *and the* when; *it should avoid venturing into the* why *and the* how. Once again, an objective is a statement of results to be achieved. It is not a justification for its own existence. The *why* bridge should have been crossed before the actual writing of the objective was begun. Although no one would deny that it's important that the people affected by your objective understand the reasons why it was selected, this communication is better handled through a verbal explanation or, if necessary, a separate statement of rationale. "To increase protective services in our service area by 10 percent" identifies the result desired. "To increase protective services in our ser-

vice area by 10 percent in order to accommodate the anticipated upsurge in population" gets into justification, which does not belong in the actual statement of objective.

Similarly, the means of accomplishing an objective is not normally included in the objective statement. The *how* relates to the action plan (discussed in Chapter Seven). The objective "to increase protective services in our service area by 10 percent through the addition of twenty uniformed officers" suggests that there is only one way to achieve the objective and thus automatically rules out other alternatives. Most objectives may be achieved by several acceptable approaches, the relative values of which might vary with changing circumstances.

The important thing to bear in mind in relation to this particular guideline is to strive toward keeping your objective statement down to its bare essentials, to keep it simple.

7. *An objective should be in direct support of, or compatible with, the organization's strategic and other high-level plans.* One of the major reasons for a tactical plan is to implement portions of strategic or high-level plans that have already been formulated. This is another check-and-balance guideline that needs to be instituted to make certain that your plan is leading your organization in a direction that is consistent with what has already been determined. This particular guideline becomes even more critical as unit plans are developed.

8. *An objective should be realistic and attainable but still represent a significant challenge.* This is a judgment call that you and your planning team must make. Any objective must have a reasonably good chance of achievement with effort that stretches the capacities of those involved; it needs to be made challenging enough so that they will feel good about themselves and the organization if and when it is achieved. At the same time, it should not be made so difficult that it is virtually impossible to achieve. Part of the value in setting objectives is to develop a sense of pride in accomplishing something that is really worthwhile. There is an adage that says, "Success begets success; failure begets failure." If your people feel good about

what they have accomplished, they are far more likely to put forth additional effort to accomplish even more. If they get the feeling that no matter how hard they try, they can never fully succeed, their incentive for top performance quickly dissipates.

Keep in mind that these guidelines are meant to provide guidance, not to be used as prescriptions. They need to be applied if and when they are appropriate. There may be times when some of these guidelines are not important, or they may not be applicable in a particular situation. If the decision to follow or not to follow particular guidelines is made with conscious awareness, it's legitimate to bypass some of them. The purpose in identifying them, however, is to make certain that key factors are not overlooked. Unfortunately, overlooking the obvious frequently causes problems in planning efforts. These guidelines are designed to reduce or eliminate that possibility. Figure 6.3 summarizes the guidelines.

Figure 6.3 Guidelines for Writing an Objective

---

1. An objective should start with the word "to" followed by an action or accomplishment verb.
2. It should specify a single measurable result to be accomplished.
3. It should specify a target date or time span for completion.
4. It should specify maximum cost factors.
5. It should be as specific and quantitative (and hence measurable and verifiable) as possible.
6. It should specify only the *what* and *when*; it should avoid venturing into the *why* and *how*.
7. It should be in direct support of, or compatible with, the organization's strategic and other high-level plans.
8. It should be realistic and attainable, but still represent a significant challenge.

Figure 6.4 includes several examples of improperly stated objectives that were subsequently revised. Included are constructive comments that led to significant improvement in the original statements. These examples demonstrate how objectives that initially are unclear or vague can be made more specific through dialogue

Figure 6.4 Examples of Restated Objectives

Original:	To decrease sales costs by 10 percent.
Comments:	Is your concern about costs associated with making the sale, product costs, service costs, inventory costs, or all of the above? Would an objective related to gross margin be more appropriate, thus enabling each related department to come up with its own contributing objectives?
Restated:	To improve gross margins in each major product line by a minimum of 10 percent by year end within existing budget.
Original:	To improve customer service.
Comments:	This is a nice statement of desire, but what does it mean? Where are there problems with customer service now— response to inquiries, deliveries, quality, follow-up? What should be happening that is not happening? Or conversely, what should not be happening that is happening? There may be room for several unit objectives here depending on each unit's specific role.
Restated:	To complete a telephone survey of at least 35 percent of customers within ten days of product delivery to determine levels of customer satisfaction and ways in which service can be improved, beginning February 1, at a weekly cost not to exceed one hundred work-hours.
Original:	To build a strong unit team.
Comments:	Great idea, but what does this mean? Are you looking for mutual commitment to unit plans, active support in backing each other up, a united front in dealing with customers? What would represent evidence that you are moving in the right direction?
Restated:	To reach agreement by March 31 with each team member on an individual plan to provide "as needed" support to at least two other team members at a training cost not to exceed forty work-hours per individual.
Original:	To acquire a new company.
Comments:	Are you interested primarily in a new or expanded manufacturing capability, additional product lines, a particular service capability, access to additional markets, or a financial investment? You need to clarify the specific

---

Figure 6.4 Examples of Restated Objectives, Cont'd.

---

results you are looking for in order to develop a meaningful action plan. Is the urgency of your need such that acquisition is clearly the most appropriate course of action, rather than developing some thing from scratch?

Restated: To acquire the capability of producing proven products (with minimum annual sales of $2,000,000) that support our service business by the end of the third quarter at a capital investment not to exceed $2,500,000.

Original: To produce more products of higher quality.

Comments: Does this mean improving the quality of current products, changing the mix between standard and premium products, producing new products at a higher quality level? How will you know you have them?

Restated: To increase production of premium quality products from 40 percent to 60 percent of total production, while maintaining current production levels of standard products, by September 30, at a conversion cost not to exceed $150,000 and five thousand work-hours.

Original: To expand our technical capability by hiring new personnel and/or cross-training existing personnel.

Comments: What results are you looking for? This statement focuses more on methodology than on accomplishment. What will be an indication of successful achievement?

Restated: To have at least three people qualified in each identified technical discipline by March 31 at a cost not to exceed two additional personnel (with related hiring costs) and eight hundred supervisory and training hours.

Original: To increase the number of active clients by at least 10 percent.

Comments: What does "active clients" mean? Is it related to frequency of contact, average or minimum revenue, categories of service? Will the increase include making up for any client losses during the year?

Restated: To increase the total number of clients with minimum annual billings of $10,000 by at least 10 percent by year end at a cost not to exceed $25,000 and five hundred contact hours.

Figure 6.4 Examples of Restated Objectives, Cont'd.

Original: To improve interdepartmental relations.

Comments: Is this objective related to departments who are your internal customers? If so, do both they and the people in your department recognize and accept that relationship? What would be an indication that this is happening?

Restated: To reach agreement on objectives related to meeting specific mutual needs, by March 31, with at least three departments we serve. (Cost is not a significant factor here.)

Original: To improve clerical effectiveness.

Comments: What is "effectiveness"? How will you know when you get there? What tells you it needs improving?

Restated: To respond to at least 95 percent of all customer correspondence within three days, effective April 30, at no increase in clerical expense, implementation cost not to exceed sixty work-hours.

---

among members of your planning team. A major responsibility of the coach/facilitator (when it is appropriate to use one) is to drive the process until the objectives stated represent clear, measurable results that reflect what you wish to accomplish during a particular planning period. Recognize, of course, that the sample objectives in the figure were relevant for the organizations for which they were written and are not necessarily appropriate for other similar organizations.

In Summary

Objectives represent the focal point of any plan.

- The three prior elements in the process—key results areas, critical issue analysis, and key performance indicators—provide the information base from which your objectives may be formulated.

- The next element—action plans—establishes the means by which your objectives will be met.

- Objectives are the principal factors by which your unit's performance may be measured.

- It is crucial that your objectives are set on the *right* things and that they are realistic and attainable.

- Most well-stated objectives follow the model *to* (action/ accomplishment verb) (single measurable result) *by* (target date/time span) *at* (cost).

- Six to ten objectives with written action plans is an appropriate number for most organizational units. This limitation will force you to concentrate on the vital few accomplishments needed.

- Other ongoing results, such as financial or production results, may be projected as standards of performance to be attained and maintained.

Once you have established a preliminary set of objectives, the next element you need to consider is action plans, which help test and validate your objectives as well as spell out how your objectives will be accomplished. These are the subject of the next chapter.

CHAPTER SEVEN

How Will You Reach Your Targets?

Preparing Your Action Plans

Okay, you've decided what your objectives should be. But, up to this point they are just wishful thinking. Suppose you plan to go on a trip. The first thing you have to determine is where you are going and when you want to arrive. However, you have several other key decisions to make if your trip is to be successful. These include your means of transportation, the route you will follow, those who will be traveling with you, where you will stay, and many other considerations. These choices may come almost as second nature to you if you are a seasoned traveler, but if you fail to give serious attention to even one of these key factors, you may end up with an unsatisfactory or even disastrous trip. Drawing on this analogy, objectives tell you where you are going and when you will arrive, while action plans show you how to get there.

What Are Action Plans?

Action plans are the specific means by which you accomplish your objectives. They also represent the point in the planning process where you need to get those who will actually implement the plans actively involved, whether or not they were involved in the earlier planning stages. While hundreds of books and articles have been written on the subject, each with its own terminology, action plans basically incorporate these five factors:

1. The specific steps or actions that will be required
2. The people who will be held accountable for seeing that each step or action is completed
3. The timetable for carrying out the steps or actions
4. The resources that will need to be allocated in order to carry them out
5. The feedback mechanisms that will be used to monitor progress within each action step

Most action plans, regardless of how simple or complex the objective, contain between five and ten major action steps. Fewer than five may indicate that insufficient consideration has been given to the amount of effort required. More than ten suggests that more detail may have been included than is appropriate.

What Is the Purpose of an Action Plan?

The first and foremost purpose of an action plan is to clearly *identify what has to take place* if you are to accomplish your objective. While this may seem obvious, the importance of this consideration becomes dramatically apparent when you discover you have overlooked something important. Ironically, it is rarely the unusual occurrence that causes significant problems in the accomplishment of an objective. More frequently, such failure occurs because someone simply didn't do something that is normally expected. For example, think of the number of times that an important project may have been delayed or even aborted because someone failed to make an important telephone call, a special test was overlooked, a vital piece of information or a key part failed to arrive on time, or someone who is usually reliable failed to keep a commitment. Your action plan helps you make certain that the obvious is not overlooked.

Another purpose for your action plan is to *test and validate* your objective. We often establish objectives based on the results desired, with no real assurance that they are truly achievable. Once you have established your draft objective, you need to break it down into smaller pieces of action to determine if you can really do it. Your action plan creates a more rational basis for determining whether

- Your objective can be reasonably accomplished within the time projected
- You have the necessary knowledge and skill to carry out the plan
- You either have or can get the necessary resources
- You can access all necessary information
- You have other alternatives that need to be considered

The development of your detailed action plan may lead you to the conclusion that your objective is unrealistic. This could result in a decision to modify your objective, modify your action plan, or postpone or even abandon your objective. The decision not to pursue an objective at this point is just as valid as a go-ahead, and it is considerably less expensive and traumatic to make such a decision before you invest significant effort.

A third purpose for your action plan is to *serve as a communications vehicle* for others who need to contribute to or who will be affected by what takes place. This is especially important when several different parts of the organization have a distinct role to play in the achievement of your objective. When you fix specific accountability for each of your action steps, there is less likelihood of delays or voids. Furthermore, communicating with others as you develop or interpret your action plan can help motivate and establish ownership among those who can make or break the outcome of your objective.

How Do You Develop Your Action Plan?

Your action plan is usually determined by using one or a combination of the following three approaches:

1. *A series of specific activities or events*, not necessarily inter-related, which will lead to the accomplishment of your objective. For example, an objective related to the implementation of a new service might include separate activities related to training those who will provide the service, orienting those who will receive the service, preparing support materials, scheduling implementation efforts, and any other activities that may have an impact on the effective implementation of the new service. Presumably, success-fully carrying out each of these activities, either independently or in combination with others, will lead to the successful accomplish-ment of your objective.

2. *An analytical or problem-solving approach*, which includes a series of interconnected events. Through this process, you first have to clearly identify the problems to be overcome or the circum-stances to be changed; you then analyze these to determine appro-priate courses of action, which are implemented sequentially, leading to the eventual accomplishment of your objective. For example, an objective related to increasing market share could start with identifying your principal competitors and what it is about their products and their approach that is providing them with a competitive advantage. Then you can initiate specific, interrelated plans to either overcome or counterbalance these factors, leading eventually to the accomplishment of your objective.

3. *A series of smaller or shorter-term objectives* that break the objective down into smaller pieces of the larger result. A common example of this type of plan is the quarterly and monthly sales fig-ures required to achieve an annual sales objective. You can also break objectives down by region, product line, specific market, or a variety of other indicators that might be worth tracking.

Figure 7.1 shows an effective method for developing your action plan.

What Is a Format That Works?

I refer to this method as an action plan *format*, not a *form*. A for-mat helps you identify the key factors that need to be included in

---

Figure 7.1 Action Planning Method

---

1. Identify suggested actions in response to the following questions.
   - What activities or results are likely to contribute to the accomplishment of this objective?
   - What specific problems, obstacles, or issues need to be resolved in order to accomplish this objective?
   - What is the sequence of events required to resolve these issues?
   - How might this objective be broken down (such as by time period, department/unit, responsibility level, or geographical region)?
2. Determine what combination of these actions is most appropriate for accomplishing this objective at this time.
3. Translate these actions into a series of five to ten major steps, with each step focusing on a specific result that may become a smaller or shorter-term objective for you or someone else.
4. For each action step, determine
   - Who will be held accountable—primary and others
   - When it should be started and completed
   - How much money and time will be required
   - How and when you will know whether you are on or off track
5. Review your proposed action plans with others who play a key role in order to test and validate the plan as well as to gain their agreement and support.

---

your plan. It should be flexible enough so you can modify it to meet the information needs of those who will be using it. Conversely, a form is usually designed to respond to a prescribed reporting system and consequently tends to be more rigid. Figure 7.2 shows a very simple format that you can use in laying out a meaningful action plan. The purpose of preparing an action plan using this type of format is to provide the *visibility* you need to get the job done in the most effective and efficient manner. Therefore, make certain the piece of paper you create does not get in the way of the process.

Here is a brief description of what is included under each of the headings in Figure 7.2:

- *Objective:* The specific objective for which the action plan is being prepared.

Objective:

Action Steps	Accountability		Schedule		Resources		Feedback Mechanisms
	Primary	Others	Start	Complete	Money	Time	

Copyright © 1995 by Jossey-Bass Publishers, San Francisco. From *Morrisey on Planning: A Guide to Long-Range Planning*, by George L. Morrisey. Permission to reproduce is hereby granted.

Figure 7.2 Action Plan Format

- *Action steps:* The five to ten major actions or events required to achieve this objective.

- *Accountability:* The specific individuals (or units) who will be held accountable for seeing that each action step is carried out. *Primary* represents the one who has ultimate accountability for completion of the step; *others* represents anyone else with a key role to play in the particular step. (There will always be the name of a unit or individual in the *primary* column; there may or may not be names in the *others* column.)

- *Schedule:* The total time frame within which the action step is to be carried out. *Start* identifies when the action must begin; *complete* identifies when that action or event must be completed.

- *Resources:* The total estimated costs for completing each of the action steps. *Money* includes all costs other than employee time, such as equipment, materials, systems, and supplies; *time* covers the amount of employee time (usually in hours or days) required to complete each action step. Time is separated from money in order to provide data for scheduling and for determining staffing needs.

- *Feedback mechanisms:* The specific methods that are available (or need to be developed) for providing the information required to track progress within each step. Feedback mechanisms can be as simple as an informational meeting or memo or as involved as the development of an information system to produce specific reports. (See the next chapter for a more detailed discussion of this aspect of planning.)

While you may condense the data included on the worksheet when your final plan is prepared, completion of such a worksheet will help ensure that you have not overlooked any key factors in the plan. Figure 7.3 shows a possible action plan for a top-level objective in a medium-size manufacturing company; Figure 7.4 illustrates an action plan for a supporting-unit objective. Figures 7.5 and

Objective: To increase productivity from 120 to 130 units per hour by December 31 at cost not to exceed $35,000

Action Steps	Accountability		Schedule		Resources		Feedback Mechanisms
	Primary	Others	Start	Complete	Money	Time	
1. Complete study of manufacturing operations, identifying areas of potential productivity improvement	Industrial Engineering	Unit Supervisors	1/15	1/31	$2,000	80 hrs	Completed report with recommendations
2. Establish and monitor quarterly targets for productivity improvement • First quarter: 122 • Second quarter: 124 • Third quarter: 127 • Fourth quarter: 130	VP Manufacturing		1/1 4/1 7/1 10/1	3/31 6/30 9/30 12/31			Quarterly results report and review meetings
3. Increase production volume • Punch press: 10% • Assembly: 8% • Final inspection: 8%	Production Superintendent	Unit Supervisors	2/15	3/31	3,000	100 hrs	Weekly and monthly production reports
4. Reduce out-of-stock levels of critical materials from 10% to a maximum of 5%	Purchasing Manager		3/1	6/30	2,000	80 hrs	Summary of inventory management report
5. Reduce equipment maintenance downtime from 15% to a maximum of 7%	Maintenance Supervisor	Unit Supervisors	3/1	9/15	4,000	120 hrs	Equipment performance report
6. Increase long production runs from 40% to 60% of scheduled runs	Schedule Supervisor	Unit Supervisors	3/1	9/30	1,000	120 hrs	Monthly production meetings—analysis of schedule mix
7. Complete supervisory training for ten manufacturing unit supervisors in areas of performance measurement and employee motivation	Production Superintendent	Training Coordinator	6/1	12/15	5,000	200 hrs	Memo from training director
8. Reduce total scrap levels from 4% to a maximum of 2%	Quality Assurance Manager	Unit Supervisors	9/1	11/15	5,000	80 hrs	Monthly quality scrap and rework summary

Figure 7.3 Sample Action Plan for a Medium-Size Manufacturing Company

Objective: To complete study of manufacturing operations, identifying areas of potential productivity improvement by January 31 at cost not to exceed $2,000 and 80 work-hours

Action Steps	Accountability		Schedule		Resources		Feedback Mechanisms
	Primary	Others	Start	Complete	Money	Time	
1. Design study approach and enlist support of unit supervisors	Industrial Engineering	Unit Supervisors	1/15	1/16		10 hrs	Completed design and agreements with unit supervisors
2. Develop computer model for completing analysis of current operations	Industrial Engineering	Data Processing	1/16	1/18	$2,000	20 hrs	Completed model
3. Complete study of punch press	Industrial Engineering	Unit Supervisor	1/21	1/22		12 hrs	Completed study
4. Complete study of assembly	Industrial Engineering	Unit Supervisor	1/24	1/25		12 hrs	Completed study
5. Complete study of final inspection	Industrial Engineering	Unit Supervisor	1/28	1/29		12 hrs	Completed study
6. Complete analysis of study results including recommendations	Industrial Engineering		1/29	1/30		8 hrs	Completed analysis
7. Present results and recommendations for improvement targets	Industrial Engineering	VP Manufacturing Unit Supervisors	1/31	1/31		3 hrs	Recommendations accepted and implemented

Figure 7.4 Sample Action Plan for Industrial Engineering

77

Objective: To reduce the number of vehicular accidents on city streets by a minimum of 5 percent over prior year's level at an implementation cost not to exceed $15,000

| Action Steps | Accountability | | Schedule | | Resources | | Feedback Mechanisms |
	Primary	Others	Start	Complete	Money	Time	
1. Determine locations of highest incidence and select those with highest potential for improvement	Traffic Engineer	Police	9/1	9/15		40 hrs	Special report summarizing high-incidence areas
2. Set up ad hoc committee to analyze and recommend corrective actions, including but not limited to • Education • Increased surveillance • Traffic control equipment • Possible rerouting	Assistant City Manager	Traffic Engineer Police City Planning Citizens	9/15	10/15	$ 500	60 hrs	Names of committee members; first meeting minutes
3. Establish information/motivation plan for police officers	Police		10/15	11/15	250	20 hrs	Copy of plan
4. Inform City Council, City Manager, other related departments, and the media about plans and progress	Assistant City Manager		10/15	12/15	250	20 hrs	Memo outlining plans and progress
5. Test proposed plans in selected locations	Traffic Engineer	Police	11/15	12/15	500	100 hrs	Monthly accident report
6. Establish monitoring system	Assistant City Manager	Data Processing Traffic Engineer Police	11/15	Ongoing	1,000	100 hrs	Copy of special detailed accident report for selected areas
7. Implement plans	Traffic Engineer	Public Relations Police	1/1	Ongoing	1,000	40 hrs per mo	Memo to announce kickoff date for new system
8. Evaluate and modify implementation	Assistant City Manager	Ad hoc committee	4/1	5/1	500	60 hrs	Quarterly management meeting to evaluate results

Figure 7.5 Sample Action Plan for a Medium-Size City

Objective: To determine locations of highest vehicular accident incidence and select those with highest potential for improvement by 9/15 at a cost not to exceed forty work-hours

Action Steps	Accountability		Schedule		Resources		Feedback Mechanisms
	Primary	Others	Start	Complete	Money	Time	
1. Study accident records for past year to determine high-incident locations	Traffic Engineer	Police	9/1	9/2		8 hrs	List of high-incidence locations
2. Visit targeted high-incident locations, observe and analyze traffic patterns	Traffic Engineer		9/3	9/5		16 hrs	Analysis summary
3. Summarize completed analyses, including review with Police, and prepare recommendations	Traffic Engineer	Police	9/8	9/10		12 hrs	Summary and recommendations completed
4. Present results and recommendations for improvement targets	Traffic Engineer	Assistant City Manager	9/14	9/14		2 hrs	Recommendations accepted and implemented

Figure 7.6 Sample Action Plan for a Traffic Engineer

7.6 represent similar types of action plans for a medium-size city. These plans are for illustrative purposes only and will not necessarily be appropriate for other, similar objectives.

What Factors Do You Need to Review in the Formulation of Your Action Plan?

As a final step before proceeding with your action plan, you may wish to check over the following factors to see if any that will impact your action plan have been overlooked. (I have included this list of factors as a checklist in Figure 7.7 with space for you to add other factors that you might identify.)

- *Strategic and/or tactical plan impact.* Are there other portions of your plans that might be positively or negatively impacted by what you will do? Can some of your action steps support other objectives as well?

- *Financial impact.* What are the capital investment or short-term cash flow implications? Are current economic conditions, such as interest rates, conducive to proceeding with your projected plan?

- *Resource availability.* Do you have or can you get the necessary skilled personnel, raw materials, information, distribution channels, and other resources to support your plan?

- *State of the art.* Could changing technology make your plan obsolete prematurely? Are you sufficiently up-to-date on what is happening technologically so you can adjust your plans accordingly?

- *Environmental conditions.* Have you taken into consideration such things as climate, weather, natural resources, and peculiar geographical circumstances that may have a positive or negative impact on your plan?

- *Political sensitivities.* Are you able to adjust your plans rapidly in order to respond more quickly to major political shifts in

the locales where you operate? Are you sensitive to the interests of key customers, board members, parent organization,
key executives, regulatory agencies, and the media, and to
public opinion in general?

- *Contractual requirements.* Are there customer or labor contracts or other legal commitments that may require a different
  course of action than would be appropriate if such contracts
  did not exist?

- *Calendar- or fiscal-year events.* Could such events as stock-
  holder meetings, industrywide new-model introductions,
  major holidays, trade shows, and other activities positively or
  negatively impact your plans?

- *Contingency plans.* Do you have a provision for contingency or
  backup plans in case something unexpected happens?

Figure 7.7 Action Plan Review Factor Checklist

Check off any of the listed factors that you need to investigate before
completing your action plans. Add any other factors that may be especially
important to you.

____ Strategic and/or tactical plan impact

____ Financial impact

____ Resource availability

____ State of the art

____ Environmental conditions

____ Political sensitivities

____ Contractual requirements

____ Calendar- or fiscal-year events

____ Contingency plans

____ _____

____ _____

____ _____

The purpose in describing these various factors is to draw your attention to the need for identifying special considerations when developing your action plans. As indicated earlier, there are many other factors that may be appropriate to your particular type of organization. Creating a list of these factors should not deter you from proceeding with your plans, but it should reduce the likelihood of your being surprised as plans evolve.

In Summary

- Action plans describe the means by which you accomplish your objectives.
- They include the specific steps or actions required, who is accountable, when the steps will be carried out, and what resources are needed.
- They are developed using one or a combination of specific activities or events, an analytical or problem-solving approach, or a series of smaller or shorter-term objectives.
- They help test and validate your objectives.
- They serve as a communications vehicle for others in the organization.
- They provide an opportunity, because of the level of detail required, to review several special considerations, such as financial impact, state of the art, and political sensitivities.

The next chapter will expand on the feedback mechanisms identified in this chapter and help you close the loop on your planning process.

CHAPTER EIGHT

How Will You Know and What Will You Do?

Reviewing and Modifying Your Plans

You've determined your KRAs, completed your critical issue analysis, identified your KPIs, established your objectives, and developed your action plans. Now you are finished with the planning process. Right? Wrong! You need to have some way of ensuring that what you set out to accomplish actually gets translated into meaningful action that leads to results.

This chapter will highlight some of the considerations and methods that are especially useful in monitoring and reinforcing progress toward the achievement of your objectives. In traditional approaches to management, this aspect is frequently referred to as *management controlling*.

What Is the Purpose of Management Controlling?

As we look at controlling as a function of management, please recognize that its primary purpose is *to alert us when changes are needed in sufficient time to take the necessary corrective action*. If there were no need for corrective action, there would be little need for you to practice management controlling. (Corrective action, by the way, may include anything from a few "fix-its" to a complete plan revision.) We need to recognize that in any kind of complex under-

---

Some of the material in this chapter has been updated and adapted from George L. Morrisey, *Management by Objectives and Results for Business and Industry* (2nd ed.), © 1977 by Addison-Wesley. Reprinted by permission.

taking *there will be a requirement for corrective action.* The fact that corrective action may be required is not necessarily evidence that someone "screwed up." It merely means that something happened other than what was anticipated. As a manager, you need to have some means of identifying plan variances so you can make the necessary adjustments to your plan. (Management controlling, in this context, is not to be confused with organizational controls or the office of the controller, which serve a broader purpose than keeping track of progress toward the achievement of objectives.)

A Word of Caution

When establishing the means by which you will maintain the kind of oversight you will need of your progress toward your objectives, please recognize that any effort devoted to overseeing your progress is effort that you and others could be devoting to "producing" activities. An appropriate caveat to keep in mind, therefore, is *effective controlling provides for adequate oversight in a timely fashion with the least expenditure of time and effort.* The key words in this statement are *adequate, timely,* and *least expenditure. Adequate* means the minimum amount of information necessary to keep up-to-date on current status. *Timely* implies the availability of feedback in sufficient time to take whatever corrective action may be required. *Least expenditure* suggests that getting the necessary feedback should cause little or no interruption to ongoing productive effort. While this point may be perfectly obvious, don't fall into the trap of spending more time and effort monitoring and reporting on your progress than you do on executing the plan itself.

What Should You Control?

Since in line with the above caution you clearly cannot maintain oversight of everything in your plan, you need to focus your monitoring efforts on the vital few factors that fall within the four basic areas of *time, resources* (human and material), *quality,* and *quantity.*

These factors will include such things as

- The small number of employees who can produce the greatest amount of high-quality work
- The small number of employees who usually produce the largest number of errors
- The small number of employees who typically have the highest rates of accidents, absenteeism, or tardiness
- Certain operations or units that cause the biggest and most frequent bottlenecks
- Certain types of equipment that have the heaviest breakdown rates
- The few products or services that generate the greatest volume of sales
- The few products or services that create the most customer dissatisfaction
- The limited number of customers or markets that produce the greatest profit
- The limited number of customers or markets that produce the greatest number of sales or service problems
- The limited number of customers who present serious collection problems
- Certain times of the day or year that are most likely to present opportunities or problems

You could add other examples to this list, I am sure. The key to effective controlling, however, lies in your identifying that relatively small number of factors that have the greatest impact on the achievement or lack of achievement of your objectives. Then you need to focus your efforts on monitoring those areas where the risk is greatest.

How Do You Monitor Your Progress?

A simple way of approaching this task is to ask yourself three fundamental questions related to the four basic elements identified earlier, using the matrix shown in Figure 8.1.

Figure 8.1 Factors in Management Controlling

Basic Elements	What Is Likely to Change?	How and When Will You Know?	What Will You Do?
Time			
Resources			
Quality			
Quantity			

What Is Likely to Change?

In approaching this question, many of the factors identified under key performance indicators, objectives, and action plans will serve as a useful starting place. Please note that you need to be concerned with what is *likely* to change, not with what could *possibly* change. You need to look for things that are going *differently* (not necessarily rightly or wrongly) from what was projected in your plan. Once again, you should focus on the vital few factors in determining what you need to be tracking. What you will be looking for are *principal causes of variances requiring corrective action.*

Variances fall into one of four general categories. However, the labels are designed merely to help in the identification of variances, not to force them into one category or another. If these labels help in that identification, then use them; if they get in the way, then don't!

1.   *Uncertainties* are reasonable expectations that may periodically result in significant fluctuations. Internal uncertainties might include such things as absenteeism, workload, flow time, accidents, errors, or traffic. External uncertainties might relate to sales revenues, customer service requirements, customer reviews or changes, market conditions, and competitor activity. Uncertainties are reasonably predictable but not guaranteed. We need a mechanism that alerts us to when these fluctuations are serious enough to require some sort of an adjustment.

2.   *Unexpected events* are those impacting factors that may not be reasonable expectations but whose impact would be so great that we need to have contingency plans ready for dealing with them. These events might include acts of nature, a state-of-the-art breakthrough, new competition, the death or departure of a key executive, loss of a major supplier, or new government regulations. Actually, the term "unexpected events" is not quite accurate, since with rare exceptions these events should not really be unexpected. In almost every such situation, early warning signs can alert us to a potential need for change, if we know what to look for.

3.   *Failures* are stoppages or delays that are largely beyond our control. Included here would be such things as machine failures, test failures, nonreceipt of critical inputs (parts, outside survey data, governmental rulings), and failure to get anticipated approvals.

4.   *Human error* relates to human performance that is largely within our control. There are two broad kinds of human error:

- *Honest error,* which occurs when basically competent people at some point fail to perform in a competent manner, may come as a result of miscalculation, lack of sufficient knowledge or skill, lack of proper instructions, a too heavy workload, outside distractions, or interferences. It represents conscientious effort that falls short of expectations.

- *Incompetency* may come as a result of willful misdoing, gross negligence, or inability to perform the work satisfactorily.

Corrective action required under these circumstances would be substantially different from that required to deal with honest error.

The question "What is likely to change?" is designed to identify those critical factors or standards that alert us to problems, opportunities, or needed modifications before they get beyond the point of no return. Remember, we are dealing with probabilities, not with absolutes.

How and When Will You Know?

Once you determine what you need to monitor, you should decide what feedback mechanisms will provide you with the most effective and efficient overview to ensure that you stay on track. While there are almost an infinite number of such mechanisms you might use, I will highlight four that are particularly useful: *progress reviews, status reports, visual displays,* and *management by exception.*

   1.   *Progress reviews,* in my opinion, are absolutely essential to sustaining any effective planning process. These reviews need to be conducted *a minimum of once each quarter* and in many instances much more frequently than that. A progress review involves a formal assessment of actual performance against your total plan, not just those portions of it that are causing problems (which should be addressed as they occur). You need to review your progress from three perspectives:

- What is going right and what you can learn from that
- What is not going right and what you are doing about it
- What is different from what existed at the time the plan was created

The natural temptation is to pass over what is going right and concentrate solely on the crises of the moment. However, by examining objectives that are proceeding according to or better than plan, you may discover ways to leverage that performance to further improve your unit's output or even to deal with some of your problem areas more effectively. Focusing on what is going right or better than right also helps identify employees who may be deserving of special recognition. By looking at what is different you may be able to bring your plans into balance with reality by modifying, expanding, or perhaps even dropping some objectives and action plans that may no longer be consistent with your original expectations. Remember, *planning is a dynamic not a static process*. Plans provide you with a baseline from which you can make trade-off decisions, if and when that is appropriate.

2. *Status reports*, whether given verbally, electronically, or in writing, are also important feedback mechanisms for staying on top of your unit's performance. My recommendation is that written status reports be *brief* (one or two pages), in *outline* rather than narrative form, and structured to quickly *highlight* the most critical information. Standardized reporting formats, which can be either manually or electronically generated, can be very useful in keeping such reports from becoming overly time-consuming for either the generator or the receiver.

3. *Visual displays* such as line graphs, milestone charts, and problem-oriented charts that are updated on a regular basis can be very effective from a motivational standpoint as well as in providing instant visibility to the factors you are monitoring. To be truly effective, such displays must show projections that reflect probable reality rather than straight-line averaging (since most factors don't operate on a straight line) and instantly highlight variances requiring corrective action without a complicated interpretation. There are many simple yet sophisticated software programs that can help you do this.

4. *Management by exception* is a powerful approach that implies that "no news is good news." This means that you, or anyone reporting to you, agree to keep those who need to know informed of any significant variances from planned performance, with the accompanying assurance that everything else is going according to

plan. This approach requires a high level of trust from you, as the supervisor, believing that you will be kept informed of what you need to know without having to check up on it. It also means that the person reporting to you must trust you to not react emotionally to negative data if continued openness in feedback is desired. This approach, coupled with periodic progress reviews, is a very effective way of establishing and maintaining accountability with the people who must perform the work.

What Will You Do?

As mentioned earlier, the only reason for establishing this kind of a feedback process is to enable you to take corrective action when necessary. This means that corrective action needs to be seen as a positive and normal part of your job and not necessarily as evidence of poor performance. Since your performance projections are largely based on estimates, some variance in actual performance is almost inevitable. The key lies in knowing what to do and when.

There are three generic kinds of corrective action you can take once you have identified a variance that requires such action. In the relative order of their value to the effectiveness of your unit, they are *self-correcting action, management action,* and *operating action.*

1.   *Self-correcting action* can take two forms. The first occurs when variances occur within acceptable tolerances, where negatives will probably balance out with positives if left alone. An example might be an average daily output of one hundred units where a deviation of plus or minus 5 percent would be acceptable, provided a trend did not develop. Your feedback mechanisms need to highlight variances that exceed that tolerance.

The second kind of self-correcting action occurs when the person accountable for a particular action becomes aware of the variance and makes the necessary correction. Without question, this is the most effective and efficient form of corrective action that can be taken, because it places the responsibility directly on the shoulders of the person doing the work, without the intervention of a third party (you as that person's supervisor). For this to work, of course, you need to make certain that feedback information reaches the accountable person as quickly as possible.

2. *Management action* addresses the *process* that may have caused the variance to occur. The variance may be the result of inadequate or inappropriate planning, insufficient training, an unexpected event that was beyond the control of the accountable person, or new information that may require a complete or partial plan revision. Your attention in such a situation may be focused as much or more on avoiding such a variance in the future as on bringing performance back to the original or a revised target. It may be appropriate to go through the critical issue analysis process again to address current circumstances.

3. *Operating action* occurs when you, as the supervisor, identify a variance and either correct it yourself or turn it over to someone else who will handle the correction. While there will be instances when such action is appropriate because of time limitations, emergency situations, policy requirements, or specific technical know-how which only you possess, operating action is usually the least desirable way to proceed. This is because such action often addresses symptoms rather than causes and, what is potentially of more concern, it places you in the position of taking responsibility for performing work that legitimately should be performed by someone else. Also, it is almost axiomatic that the more often we solve our employees' problems for them, the more often they will let us.

In Summary

Plan review, the final element in our planning model, is designed to close the loop and keep you on track toward accomplishing what you set out to do as a part of the earlier steps. The key to making the feedback and monitoring part of the process work is to recognize that it is a human rather than a mechanical tool. You need to exercise sound managerial judgment as you ask yourself the three fundamental questions:

- What is likely to change?
- How and when will you know?
- What will you do?

Keep in mind my earlier admonition that *effective controlling provides for adequate oversight in a timely fashion with the least expenditure of time and effort.*

CHAPTER NINE

How Can You Make It Work?

Assessing and Implementing Your Planning Process

Now it's time to pull it all together in a way that will make this process work specifically for your organization. We will approach this task initially from the perspective of the total organization and then show a more simplified approach for developing and implementing a unit plan. In your role as unit president, you need to determine what portions of each approach make the most sense for you. To make your planning process truly effective, you need to *adapt*, not adopt, this or any other approach to planning. Keeping your own unique requirements in mind, here are some special considerations that can make planning work more effectively in your organization.

Where Are You with Your Planning?

Whether you recognize it or not, you already have a plan of some sort. It may be located primarily in your mind and/or the minds of one or more additional members of management. It may range anywhere from a complete detailed plan to a budget to a sales plan to a "to do" list. The point is that you don't have to start over; you can begin wherever you are now in the planning process. In assessing your current process, you need to answer three basic questions to determine what changes may be needed:

1. *Is your current planning process doing the job?* Does it clearly identify what needs to be accomplished for your organization

to be successful? Does the plan lead to the kinds of effort that produce the results you need?

2. *Is your current planning effort organization-wide in application?* Does it involve all managers and key employees in a planning effort that is integrated both vertically and horizontally? (Note: if it is not organization-wide at present, you can still proceed within your own "company" as unit president while influencing others to follow a similar approach.)

3. *How can your current planning process be strengthened?* What parts of the process, or of the organization, need attention to ensure greater consistency in your planning efforts?

The Planning Assessment Checklist presented in Figure 9.1 is a tool that will help you test the readiness of your organization for planning and quickly evaluate the effectiveness and completeness of your current planning practices. It provides a quick overview of what is involved in planning, together with an opportunity for pinpointing specific additions or modifications that may be required to make your approach as effective as possible. You can then take whatever actions may be required to address these various deficiencies. When approaching this process from a total organization perspective, the initial assessment normally is made by the CEO, the senior executive team, and/or the planning process facilitator. Individuals who may be given assignments related to one or more factors on the checklist need to understand and accept the responsibility for whatever action may be expected. If you are examining your planning specifically from the perspective of your own unit, then you only need to examine those factors that are relevant to your plan.

In making the assessment, you need to go through the checklist and place a check in the appropriate column for each item. OK means that your current planning process addresses that item satisfactorily. It may need some fine tuning, but following existing practices is likely to produce the desired results. *Need* indicates either that this item should be added or that a more effective application is required than the one you currently use. N.A. should be checked if that item is not applicable to your particular unit. After completing the initial checks, review each of the items that has a check in the *Need* column and determine what action is required by when and by whom. Figure 9.2 is an example of a checklist completed by a CEO. The checklist highlights those portions of the planning process that require special attention. It also provides a blueprint for getting started.

What Is Involved in Implementing an Organization-Wide Approach?

Remember, *organization-wide planning* implies the active involvement of managers at all levels in creating plans that are compatible with each other. This is in contrast to *top-down planning*, in which plans are created at the executive level and distributed to other managers for implementation. Here are some special considerations to keep in mind related to organization-wide planning.

- *A longer time span is required for organization-wide planning than for top-down planning.* This does not necessarily mean more managerial time. It does mean that because of the iterative nature of the process more calendar time must be allocated to allow all relevant inputs to the process to be made. Depending on the size and complexity of the organization, from initiation to final approval, planning is likely to take from two to four months of elapsed time, with three months a realistic average for a moderate-size organization.

- *Individual managerial time investment should not be excessive,* assuming that most managers are already involved at least in budget preparation. While there will be many exceptions in either direction, executives and members of upper-middle management can expect to invest anywhere from four to seven total days of group effort during the course of plan development. Normally this will include a series of meetings rather than a single, extended planning session, to allow for additional analysis that may be required as well

Figure 9.1 Planning Assessment Checklist

	Current Status			Action (When and Who)
	OK	Need	N/A	
Preplanning Factors				
Planning Process Model				
Planning Roles Clarified				
• CEO				
• Senior Management Team				
• Unit President				
• Unit Planning Team				
• Planning Facilitator				
Review of Current Plans				
Plan to Plan				
Tactical Planning				
Key Results Areas				
Critical Issue Analysis				
• Issues Identified/Analyzed				
• Major Conclusions				
Key Performance Indicators				
Objectives (including standards)				
Action Plans				
Plan Review Process				
Additional Considerations				
Cross-Functional Coordination				
Unit Mission Statements				
Unit Tactical Plans				
Training/Coaching				
Plan Documentation				
Plan Communication				

as for the iterative process with organizational units. Lower-middle and first-line managers probably will spend less time in plan development, because their plans tend to be more clear-cut.

• *Planned information sharing, with appropriate feedback, should result in better communications.* Since organization-wide planning is

Figure 9.2 Sample Completed Planning Assessment Checklist

	Current Status			Action (When and Who)
	OK	**Need**	**N/A**	
Preplanning Factors				
Planning Process Model	✓			
Planning Roles Clarified	✓			
• CEO	✓			
• Senior Management Team	✓			
• Unit President	✓			
• Unit Planning Team		✓		Each unit president
• Planning Facilitator	✓			Bill Scott
Review of Current Plans		✓		Preplanning meeting Sept. 1: Me
Plan to Plan		✓		Preplanning meeting Sept. 1: Bill
Tactical Planning				
Key Results Areas	✓			
Critical Issue Analysis		✓		Bill prepare questionnaire Aug. 15
• Issues Identified/Analyzed		✓		First meeting
• Major Conclusions		✓		Second meeting
Key Performance Indicators		✓		Need to expand
Objectives (including standards)		✓		Need to tie in to KPIs
Action Plans	✓			
Plan Review Process		✓		I will set ground rules Sept. 1
Additional Considerations				
Cross-Functional Coordination	✓			Need to reinforce
Unit Mission Statements		✓		Each unit president
Unit Tactical Plans	✓			Modify next year
Training/Coaching		✓		Arrange training Oct. 1: Bill
Plan Documentation	✓			Modify next year
Plan Communication		✓		Bill to coordinate

dependent on the sharing of information, both vertically and horizontally, the result is better understanding of the plan and the planning process. This requires a commitment at all levels to share plans promptly with others who have a need to know.

• *Less rework of plans and budgets should be required.* In many organizations, plans and budgets are submitted, revised, and resubmitted several times before they are finally accepted. Because of the information sharing that takes place in organization-wide planning, and because the preparation of budgets is tied in so closely with the tactical plan, less rework is normally required. Managers are better informed and therefore tend to do a more realistic and accurate job of plan preparation.

- *Developing and maintaining a planning schedule is critical.* Because of the number of pieces that need to come together, a realistic schedule must be established and adhered to. An effective tool for doing this is a *Plan to Plan*. This is not just a play on words. A Plan to Plan clearly identifies significant steps in the planning process that need to be completed if planning is to be an effective management tool. The Plan to Plan highlights the specific portions of the plan that need to be developed, sets a schedule for completion of each of these portions, and establishes a record of performance against that schedule.

Figure 9.3 is a sample Plan to Plan, including provision for unit plan development. There are many variations, of course, depending on the size of your organization and the amount of unit plan development required. You need to develop your own Plan to Plan, based on your specific planning requirements. Typically, the final event in the Plan to Plan will be review and approval by whoever has the final say. Usually there is a specific time frame within which approval must take place. Approval may be by a board of directors, a parent company, a legislative body, or the CEO and the planning team themselves. By establishing a specific deadline by which approval must be obtained, it's possible to work backward and determine a realistic schedule for completion of each of the plan elements as well as for submission of unit plans.

What Is Involved in Implementing a Unit Approach?

Depending on the size of your unit, some of the considerations for the organization-wide approach may apply, or a more informal approach may work as well or better. You at least need to give some thought to the following:

Figure 9.3 Sample Plan to Plan

Objective: To complete the annual plan for next fiscal year by December 1

Action Steps	**Timetable**

1. Half-day preplanning meeting — September 1
   - Introduction to or review of process
   - Review of prior plans
   - Identification of key results areas, issues and analysis assignments

2. One-day planning meeting — September 15
   - Review of analysis assignments and agreement on issues and conclusions
   - Agreement on key performance indicators

3. Dissemination of key results areas, issues, conclusions, and key performance indicators throughout organization for review and feedback — September 16–30

4. One-day planning meeting — October 1
   - Review and modification based on feedback
   - Agreement on preliminary objectives and action plans
   - Initiation of budget process

5. Preparation and submission of unit plans and budgets — October 2–31

6. One-day planning meeting — November 1
   - Review of unit plans and budgets
   - Agreement on alternatives to achieve objectives
   - Referral of unit plans for modification

7. Half-day planning meeting — November 15
   - Agreement on final objectives, action plans, and budgets

8. Documentation of plan — November 16–30

9. One-day planning meeting — December 1
   - Review of and final agreement on plan
   - Plan for implementation and monthly/ quarterly reviews

- *Your plan needs to support, or at least be compatible with, higher-level plans.* Regardless of the form in which higher-level plans exist, you need to determine where your unit fits and what results you are expected to deliver. If this is not clear at the outset, you may have to articulate your perceptions of these expectations and review them with your immediate supervisor before investing a lot of effort in developing your plan. An advantage to you in the absence of specific higher-level plans may be the opportunity to significantly influence the direction of the organization as well as the implementation of a compatible planning process.

- *Cross-functional coordination/communication becomes especially critical at the unit level.* Since much of what you will accomplish will either impact, or be impacted by, the plans of your peer managers, it's important that you establish and maintain open lines of communication with them regarding your plans and theirs. Unit planning should be a time for cooperation and coordination, not for competition.

- *Active involvement of the people in your unit is essential to the success of your plan.* Assuming that you have employees reporting to you, this is a marvelous opportunity to get both their inputs and their buy-in to your unit's plan. This is also an excellent way to build teamwork among your group as you focus together on what your unit needs to accomplish.

- *Your time and the time of your people will probably be spent more informally than formally, although some meetings will be required.* Some of your planning effort will be one-on-one with your direct reports and some will benefit from group interaction. You need to determine what combination of these works best for you. If there is a set time for budget submission in your organization, you need to schedule your planning efforts well in advance of that deadline so you can do your planning with less pressure.

What Does a Plan Look Like?

Clients frequently ask, "How many pages should be in our plan?" A true but unsatisfactory answer would be, "As many as you need to get the job done." While there is no magic formula, I frequently recommend between fifteen and twenty-five pages for a medium-size organization. (Figure 9.4 shows a sample table of contents for one such company. Please recognize that, while this plan was appropriate for this particular company, it probably will not be appropriate for your organization.) Whatever is included in the organizational plan should reflect only what will impact the total organization. Specific departmental or unit plans usually will be considerably shorter and more specific. Unit plans may or may not be retained at a central location for reference purposes. However, I recommend

Figure 9.4 Sample Table of Contents for a Company's Tactical Plan

	Pages
1. Executive Overview	1–2
2. Key Results Areas • Profitability • Market expansion • New product development • Quality • Customer service • Employee development	3
3. Critical Issue Analysis: Issues and Conclusions • New markets needed to meet growth goals • Redesign of products to address technological obsolescence • Need to improve customer satisfaction/service	4–7
4. Key Performance Indicators	8
5. Objectives (including standards of performance)	9
6. Action Plans	10–15
7. Budget Summaries (developed separately) • Revenue • Expense • Capital • Cash flow	16–19
8. Plan Implementation and Review Schedule	20

against including them in the total organizational plan as that will tend to dilute its impact or invite unnecessary scrutiny of unit efforts. The total organization's plan should be a living document that is familiar to all key people within the organization and is reviewed formally on a regular basis. This cannot and will not be done with a large volume of material. Remember Morrisey's Law: *the utility of any planning document is in inverse relationship to its length.*

Once the plan for the total organization has been documented and approved, it's important that all key people throughout the organization be made aware of its content and importance. While it will not necessarily be appropriate to distribute the entire plan throughout the organization, it's usually desirable to circulate an executive overview, which summarizes the key elements of the plan, to everyone with a need to know. Specific portions of the plan may also be discussed at some length in meetings of departments or units that have implementation responsibility for those portions. A scaled-down version of this approach may be appropriate at the unit level as well.

When May Strategic and Tactical Planning Be Completed Together?

As has been pointed out several times in this book, organizational planning is generally much more effective when strategic and tactical planning are separated. However, in certain situations, such as the following, it may be either necessary or desirable to approach them simultaneously.

• If your organization is embarking on a formal planning process for the first time, it may not be feasible for you to complete both the strategic and tactical plans as distinctly separate efforts at different times. Recognizing that much of the initial effort is likely to be placed on your annual plan in such a situation, it may be appropriate to address such things as organization mission and strategy as a preliminary effort to determining appropriate results for the coming year. The identification of critical issues, which can be incorporated as an early step, may address factors that have both strategic and tactical significance. This simultaneous planning should be perceived as a temporary aberration that needs to be adjusted when a normal planning cycle can be instituted.

• A major unexpected event that causes a significant change in direction for the organization may require substantial modification of the strategic plan while tactical plans are being developed, in order to meet short-term needs as well as address long-term concerns. For example, such things as technological breakthroughs, unexpected new competition, restrictive legislation, or major crises (such as wars, boycotts, or critical shortages) may require an immediate modification of the organization's concept and direction. This modification may be a temporary adjustment or a complete and permanent change.

When circumstances suggest that both strategic and tactical planning be addressed at the same time, your planning process facilitator needs to make certain that discussion of strategic issues is not overly cluttered with tactical concerns. Even if the planning effort must be completed in a concentrated series of meetings, strategic elements such as organization mission and strategy should be formulated before specific objectives are determined.

What Is Different About Planning in Public Sector Organizations?

The principles and practices of effective planning are as applicable to governmental organizations as they are to companies in the private sector. The differences between the two kinds of organizations are far more in degree than they are in kind. Some of these differences, however, may need special attention. For example:

• The budget cycle in governmental organizations tends to have significantly longer lead times than in most companies in the private sector. This means that annual plans may have to be completed several months before what might be an ideal time. It also may mean that greater consideration must be given to contingency plans in the event that certain assumptions turn out to be invalid. For example, an unanticipated change in the economy could significantly alter the demand for welfare assistance from what was projected when plans were prepared.

• The legislative process and the political ramifications associated with it are likely to influence the way plans are prepared and submitted for approval. For example, certain objectives an agency might wish to set that have strong political overtones could receive greater or lesser support during an election year than they might during a nonelection year.

• The media tend to have considerably more interest in reviewing and analyzing plans prepared by governmental agencies than those prepared by private corporations. So-called investigative reporters frequently look for proposed efforts that have "headline potential." Since in most cases governmental agency plans are in the public domain, some organizations may want to temper language and avoid certain details which, if taken out of context, could be misinterpreted by the public.

• Jurisdictional disputes over which agency should have responsibility for a particular effort may become particularly sensitive because of political factors. A clear statement of mission that is approved by the appropriate legislative body should at least reduce the potential of such jurisdictional disputes.

What About Management by Objectives?

Management by Objectives—or as I refer to it, Management by Objectives and Results (MOR)—is directed more at individual managerial efforts than at those of the total organization. The two efforts are very clearly related, but they are not designed to accomplish the same purpose. MOR can be used to draw a distinction between your individual projected accomplishments and those of your unit. The manager who says, "My unit's objectives are my objectives" is only partially correct. Although you will be held accountable for the results that are to be produced within your unit, certain KRAs, such as coaching and counseling, organizational relationships, and managerial responsibilities, may need to be separated from your unit's plan. MOR is a powerful motivational tool for individual managers that is totally compatible with the approach to planning described in this book. It is also useful as a basis for performance appraisal. (For further information on the use of MOR, please refer to my related texts, described in the Annotated Resources.)

In Summary

The assessment and implementation of your tactical planning process helps you to

- Determine where you currently are with your planning process
- Determine what additions or modifications in your process are needed
- Define what your organization or unit intends to accomplish during the coming year, and when and how this will take place
- Implement the coming year's portion of your strategic plan
- Enlist the active involvement of all who must play a role in the process
- Establish an appropriate review process to ensure that plans are implemented

Strategic planning is visionary and long-range. Tactical planning is specific and short-term. They must be coordinated to ensure an effective, results-producing planning process. The key to success in the planning process lies in getting the active involvement and commitment of everyone in the organization. Remember, the purpose of planning is not primarily to produce plans; it is to produce results, and this requires total organizational commitment.

Appendix

Developing Your Unit's Roles and Missions

As indicated several times throughout this book, a statement of roles and missions for your work unit is an important foundation document in the development of your unit's plan. Naturally, this statement must support the mission of your total organization. There are, however, some distinct differences in the statement of a specific unit. For example, I refer to the unit statement as a statement of roles and missions rather than of mission alone. This focus will help you to identify the variety of specific roles your unit may play or tasks it may perform in support of your total organization's mission, such as designing, testing, analyzing, manufacturing, or selling. It's not necessary, however, to separate roles and missions in your statement, because they overlap and are both part of your unit's commitments. Also, each unit's statement must be clearly separate from other units' statements. No two units within a total organization should have identical roles and missions. If they do, the organization is inviting duplication of effort or, what may be worse, an effort gap.

Why Should There Be a Statement of Roles and Missions for Each Separate Unit?

There are several reasons why each unit should have its own statement of roles and missions. Some of the more important factors are:

Note: this supplement is a slight adaptation of Chapter Five from the first book in this series, *A Guide to Strategic Thinking.* It is included here to assist those managers who may not be directly involved in determining strategic direction for the total organization but who will benefit from having a clear statement of roles and missions for their units.

- To ensure that all critical work is accomplished and that accountability is established for it, thus avoiding the problems that occur when everyone assumes that somebody else is doing it
- To reduce, if not eliminate, the likelihood of duplication of effort
- To ensure that individual employees within your unit clearly see the relationship between what they are doing and the apparent reasons for the existence of the total organization
- To ensure that effort is being expended on work that clearly contributes to, and does not detract from, the economic well-being of the total organization
- To reduce the likelihood of jurisdictional disputes among related organizational units
- To serve as a forum for resolution of misunderstandings or disputes within each unit as well as among related units

While a clear statement of roles and missions will not guarantee that these various factors will be addressed appropriately, the absence of such a statement will inevitably lead to some of the negative consequences implied. In addition, of course, a valid statement of roles and missions is the baseline from which all your unit's objectives should be drawn. In other words, any objective you project should be in direct support of your unit's statement of roles and missions; otherwise, serious questions should be raised as to whether any significant effort should be devoted to that objective at all.

Where Does My Unit's Statement of Roles and Missions Originate?

Ideally, a clear, concise, and comprehensive statement of mission for the total organization provides the basis for roles and missions statements of smaller units within it. If no organization-wide statement exists, however, you must create one, at least conceptually, before your unit's roles and missions can be defined. A similar definition may be required if your unit is part of a larger unit such as a division or department that does not have its own mission statement.

Figure A.1 contains a series of questions for clarifying organizational unit roles and missions. They are similar to those for the total

---

Figure A.1 Questions for Clarifying Unit Roles and Missions

1. What business is the total organization in? Why does it exist?
2. What business is my unit in?
3. Why does my unit exist (what is our basic purpose)?
4. Who are my unit's principal customers/clients/users? Are we primarily a production or support operation?
5. What are my unit's principal products/services/functions?
6. How do these products/services/functions contribute to the total organization's mission?
7. What is unique or distinctive about my unit's work compared to that of other units in the organization?
8. How is my unit's work different from what it was three to five years ago?
9. What is likely to be different about my unit's work three to five years in the future?
10. What should be my unit's economic commitment to the total organization?
11. What philosophical issues, values, and priorities are important to my unit's future (related to organization and/or department image, customers, employees, safety, environment, innovation/risk taking, administrative practices, and so on)?
12. What special considerations do we have (if not addressed above) in regard to:
    - Upper management?
    - Customers/clients/users?
    - Employees?
    - Suppliers?
    - Peer organizations?
    - General public?
    - Others (specify)?

---

organization (covered in Chapter Four of *A Guide to Strategic Thinking*) but are focused at the unit level.

How Should Unit Statements Be Prepared?

I recommend the following step-by-step process as a logical method for defining your unit's statement of roles and missions. Whether or not you follow each step precisely is a matter of choice and depends on your circumstances.

1. Identify the total organization's mission (either from its formal statement or by your own analysis).

2. Identify the roles and missions of the major department or functional unit of which you are a part.

3. Determine appropriate answers to those questions posed in Figure A.1 that are relevant for you. (If possible, involve your key employees in this discussion and analysis.)

4. Prepare a rough draft of your roles and missions statement.

5. Check your draft statement against the key questions for evaluating unit roles and missions listed in the next section. Force yourself to analyze the draft objectively. Invite others to assist you in the process.

6. Review the draft in depth with your immediate supervisor, your key employees, and any peer managers to whom it would be relevant. Modify the draft as appropriate.

Key Questions for Evaluating Unit Roles and Missions

The following questions should be used to validate or further modify your draft statement of unit roles and missions before final acceptance:

1. Does the statement include all *pertinent* commitments (for example, economic, functional, product, service, market, and geographical)?
2. Is there a clear determination of production or support relationship?
3. Is the statement unique or distinctive in some way?
4. Is it consistent with, without duplicating, peer statements of roles and missions?
5. Is it understandable, brief, and concise?
6. Is the complete unit function stated and self-contained?
7. Does the statement provide a clear linkage to other related roles and missions statements?

What Are Some Examples of Unit Roles and Missions?

The following examples are actual unit statements of roles and missions of specific departments in Burger King Corporation and BHP Minerals/The San Juan Mine (which are used here with permission), as well as other statements adapted from business and governmental organizations.

Burger King Operations Standards Department

Through the establishment, maintenance, and improvement of operational standards, the Operations Standards group will seek to

- Safeguard the Burger King® brand
- Enhance customer satisfaction
- Simplify restaurant operations
- Increase consistency
- Improve restaurant profitability

Burger King Worldwide Restaurant Operations—Latin America

In support of the Burger King® mission, Worldwide Restaurant Operations—Latin America will provide franchisees and restaurants with operational and marketing support. To accomplish this, we are committed to adding value by

- Assisting in building sales and profitability in existing and new restaurants that meet or exceed company and franchisee expectations
- Providing team leadership and open communication in ensuring high standards resulting in customer satisfaction
- Being sensitive and responsive to the cultural values and needs of the communities we serve
- Establishing and enhancing sound working relationships with suppliers and other business partners

Burger King Worldwide Restaurant Operations— Europe/Middle East/Africa (WWRO-EMA)

WWRO-EMA will provide the expertise and support to enable our franchisees and restaurants to deliver the Burger King® mission through a consistent and innovative approach to

- Improving customer satisfaction
- Increasing sales, profitability, and growth
- Ensuring high standards by improving restaurant operations
- Emphasizing teamwork, Pan-EMA, amongst ourselves and our business partners

San Juan Mine Departments

Safety Department. To contribute to the mission and goals of San Juan Mine and BHP Minerals by serving as an expert resource on safety and health to all mine departments, ensuring compliance with MSHA [Mine Safety and Health Agency] and other appropriate regulatory agencies, and coordinating the emergency response and chemical control programs. In support of this, we are committed to

- Providing up-to-date dynamic materials and resources for use in training in support of our mission
- Knowing, understanding, and serving our customers' needs in a timely manner
- Representing San Juan Mine and BHP Minerals on safety and health issues in the communities in which we are involved

Supply Department. To contribute to the mission and goals of San Juan Mine by ensuring cost effective and timely purchase and distribution of required materials for internal customers. In support of this, we are committed to

- Knowing, understanding, and serving our customers' needs in a cost-effective and timely manner
- Creating and maintaining a work environment that encourages the growth and development of our employees
- Complying with all regulatory and corporate requirements, while maintaining the highest standards of ethical performance.

Engineering Department. To contribute to the mission and goals of San Juan Mine by providing innovative leadership to meet our customers' needs through effective design, planning, and technical support. In achieving this mission, our major roles are to

- Provide mine design and mine planning support
- Provide regulatory compliance design and planning support
- Provide surveying, drafting, and statistical support
- Provide strategic planning support for future growth
- Assist in the development of the technical and professional skills of staff

- Interact with external customers proactively and professionally
- Help make San Juan Mine an enjoyable place to work

Production Department. To contribute to the mission and goals of San Juan Mine by cost-effectively producing quality coal for our customers. In support of this, we are committed to

- Making safety first; production will follow
- Optimizing all production functions to support the production of quality coal
- Establishing and maintaining win-win relationships with all of our internal and external customers and suppliers
- Complying willingly with all regulatory requirements that apply to us
- Recognizing and improving the skills and performance of everyone in the department
- Creating an environment that encourages innovation and continuous improvement
- Being sensitive to the needs of the communities in which we operate

Maintenance Department. To contribute to the mission and goals of San Juan Mine by providing cost-effective quality maintenance service to our customers within an acceptable time frame. In support of this, we are committed to

- Making safety our first priority
- Complying with all regulatory requirements
- Establishing and maintaining win-win, trusting relationships with all of our internal and external customers and suppliers
- Clearly establishing expectations, recognizing individuals and holding them accountable for their performance

- Providing training and development opportunities to encourage all our employees to reach their full potential

- Continuous improvement through innovation, teamwork, training, planning, and cost management

Other Examples of Unit Roles and Missions

A *marketing department*. The roles and missions of the Marketing Department are to contribute to the profitability and growth of the ABC Corporation through the effective marketing and sales of its present and future products and services. These roles and missions will be carried out in the domestic industrial, educational, and governmental markets through direct sales and franchised dealers. This department exists in order to

- Pinpoint and maintain contact with widely scattered specialized markets throughout the United States

- Identify, qualify, and maintain contact with current and new influential buyers and decision makers in our markets

- Discover new uses and markets for existing products/services and introduce new products/services effectively and economically

- Create a receptive audience for our products/services and our sales representatives

A *regional office*. The roles and missions of the Southwest Area Office are to carry out the mission of the agency in our assigned geographical area by

- Continually assessing and responding to the related needs of the people and communities being served

- Effectively interpreting the agency's mission to those being served and to the general public

- Providing constructive feedback to the agency on local acceptance of agency programs and the need for new or modified services
- Ensuring cost-effective use of available resources
- Providing opportunities for meaningful and satisfying service and personal and career growth for all area employees

A bank operations department. The roles and missions of the Operations Department are to contribute to the profitability and growth of the ABC Community Bank by providing high-quality services to the bank's customers in the following areas:

- Teller services
- Automated teller machine (ATM) services
- Bank-by-mail services
- Safe deposit services
- Contract collections
- New accounts
- Bookkeeping
- General ledger maintenance
- Monthly statements
- Cash maintenance and control
- Incoming and outgoing collections and transfers
- Clearings

The department exists in order to

- Provide bank customers with rapid, accurate, and courteous service designed to promote continuation and expansion of a banking relationship
- Protect the interests of the bank through cost-effective provision of services and by ensuring proper allocation of appropriate charges

- Promote and maintain a positive, helpful image for the bank with its customers and the general public
- Create and maintain a mutually supportive working and learning relationship among bank employees

In Summary

Although it is a strategic planning element, a statement of unit roles and missions is an especially important document for you to develop or review prior to starting your unit planning process. That is why this appendix has been included even though developing unit roles and missions is not actually a part of tactical planning. This statement provides a foundation for clearly determining the efforts to be carried out at your unit level. Addressing the critical, ongoing expectations of your unit at least once a year helps to assure that the needs of the total organization will be met.

Annotated Resources

I have found the following books useful in my study of management and planning practices. Most are recent publications, but I have also included a few classics that have influenced me greatly as I have proceeded on my own journey through the world of planning. This is not an exhaustive list. There are many other fine publications; these just happen to be ones that are meaningful to me. Since the subject matter of many of these titles overlaps the content in each of the three books in this series, the same set of annotated resources appears in each of them.

General Management and Management Tools

Applegate, Jane. *Strategies for Small Business Success*. New York: Plume/Penguin, 1995.
> This delightful book by a nationally syndicated columnist is both a compilation of some of her most popular columns and a collection of advice gathered from many small business entrepreneurs as well as from her own experience. The section on "Going Global" is especially worth reading by those who are anticipating moving into foreign markets.

Batten, Joe D. *Tough-Minded Leadership*. New York: Amacom, 1989.
> Joe Batten has been a close friend and colleague of mine for many years. As a writer and speaker, he has a unique talent for getting people to practice what they profess to believe. This book is a milestone piece of literature that provides clear direction for establishing a style of leadership that truly *expects* (and usually gets) performance that leads to outstanding results.

Bellman, Geoffrey M. *Getting Things Done When You Are Not in Charge: How to Succeed from a Support Position*. San Francisco: Berrett-Koehler, 1992.

Geoff Bellman addresses many of the frustrations that those of us who have been in support positions have experienced when trying to move our ideas through the corporate maze. We are not as powerless as we like to think we are. This book supports my concept of the *unit president*, showing practical ways of impacting organizational direction and results.

Block, Zenas, and MacMillan, Ian C. *Corporate Venturing: Create New Businesses in Your Firm*. Boston: Harvard Business School Press, 1993.
This book is designed for the internal champion, working under the corporate umbrella, who is charged with developing and marketing new ventures that are a distinct departure from the company's core products. Drawing on many real-world examples, it provides principles and techniques for making the new venture a success.

Collins, James C., and Porras, Jerry I. *Built to Last: Successful Habits of Visionary Companies*. New York: HarperCollins, 1994.
This book is a fascinating summary of research done with several companies the authors describe as *visionary* relative to several other successful but less-visionary companies in the same industries, all of which were founded before 1950. The "Twelve Shattered Myths" (such as "It takes a great idea to start a great company" and "Visionary companies require great and charismatic visionary leaders"), which are the theme of the book, provide eye-opening insights as well as methodologies for determining what makes the most sense for the future of your company.

Conner, Daryl R. *Management at the Speed of Change: How Resilient Managers Succeed and Prosper Where Others Fail*. New York: Villard Books, 1995.
Daryl Conner has been both a pioneer and a continual student in the field of change management. This book embodies the essence of his experience in working with a wide range of organizations as they move in dramatic new directions.

Drucker, Peter F. *Managing for the Future: The 1990s and Beyond*. New York: Truman Talley Books/Dutton, 1992.
Peter Drucker continues to be one of the world's most influential management thinkers, frequently years ahead of his time. This book presents a series of provocative and insightful essays under four broad headings: "Economics," "People," "Management," and "The Organization." "The Trend Toward Alliances for Progress" is a brief but precise set of guidelines for addressing one of the major business trends of the future.

Hammer, Michael, and Stanton, Steven E. *The Reengineering Revolution: A Handbook*. New York: HarperCollins, 1995.

This new book from the coauthor of *Reengineering the Corporation* addresses many of the successes and problems that have occurred within organizations that have undertaken reengineering efforts. It will be especially helpful to those managers who are seriously considering reengineering as a change methodology but who don't wish to get caught up in a "bandwagon" approach.

Leibfried, Kathleen H. J., and McNair, C. J. *Benchmarking: A Tool for Continuous Improvement.* New York: HarperCollins, 1992.
This book from The Coopers & Lybrand Performance Solutions Series is the most comprehensive publication on the subject that I have seen. It emphasizes the importance of using this approach as *a never-ending objective* in maintaining the competitive edge.

Naisbitt, John. *Global Paradox: The Bigger the World Economy, the More Powerful Its Smallest Players.* New York: Morrow, 1994.
John Naisbitt, of *Megatrends* fame, addresses the trend toward dramatic change in the ways that companies and countries do business. His premise is that "huge companies like IBM, Philips, and GM must break up to become confederations of small, autonomous, entrepreneurial companies if they are to survive." This is provocative reading from one of the foremost futurists of our time.

Osborne, David, and Gaebler, Ted. *Reinventing Government: How the Entrepreneurial Spirit Is Transforming the Public Sector.* Reading, Mass: Addison-Wesley, 1992.
This is not a government-bashing treatise. It is a rational approach to using modern management principles and techniques to address the unique management concerns of government operations. The book is amply illustrated with examples of governmental entities that are doing this successfully at the national, state, and local levels.

Schmidt, Warren H., and Finnegan, Jerome P. *TQManager: A Practical Guide for Managing in a Total Quality Organization.* San Francisco: Jossey-Bass, 1993.
Warren Schmidt and Jerry Finnegan have boiled down to the basics the concepts and competencies of the total-quality approach, without all the hoopla. If you want to learn how to make TQM work, this is the book to read.

Planning Theory and Practice

Allen, Louis A. *Making Managerial Planning More Effective.* New York: McGraw-Hill, 1982.

I had the privilege of working with Louis Allen in the mid 1960s while I was in a staff position at Rockwell International, to which he was serving as a consultant. He had a major impact on my managerial thinking and on my desire to become more involved in the planning process. This classic book provides comprehensive coverage of planning from the perspective of the individual manager rather than of the enterprise as a whole. Chapter Eight, "The Position Plan," is especially helpful for managers who need to define their own accountabilities as part of the total planning effort.

Austin, L. Allan, and Hall, Dean G. *COmpetitive REsourcing: How to Use Decision Packages to Make the Best Use of Human and Financial Assets*. New York: Amacom, 1989.

I have come to know Allan Austin as a brilliant strategic thinker with a strong international reputation. Few consultants in the field know how to address global competition as he does. This book is particularly directed toward managers in mature industries (those whose global market growth has dropped below 10 percent annually). Allan and his coauthor, Dean Hall, describe the COmpetitive REsourcing (CORE) process, which requires senior managers to identify their competitive gaps, establish strategies to reduce the gaps, and enlist the creativity and innovation needed from all levels of the organization to eliminate the gaps.

Below, Patrick J., Morrisey, George L., and Acomb, Betty L. *The Executive Guide to Strategic Planning*. San Francisco: Jossey-Bass, 1987.

This book helped establish the foundation from which the first two books in this series were derived. While I have made several modifications to the integrated planning process first introduced in *The Executive Guide*, the book still represents a sound approach to the strategic planning process.

Bryson, John M. *Strategic Planning for Public and Nonprofit Organizations: A Guide to Strengthening and Sustaining Organizational Achievement*. San Francisco: Jossey-Bass, 1988.

Recognizing that the principles and techniques of strategic planning are as important in the public and the nonprofit worlds as they are in corporate America, John Bryson shows how to make strategic planning work for city managers and administrators, cabinet secretaries, school superintendents and principals, sheriffs and police chiefs, elected and appointed officials of governments and public agencies, and boards of directors of nonprofit organizations.

de Bono, Edward. *de Bono's Thinking Course*, Rev. ed. United Kingdom: MICA Management Resources, 1994.

As de Bono says in the "Author's Note" in the book, "Thinking is the ultimate human resource. The quality of our future will depend entirely on the quality of our thinking. This applies on a personal level, a community level and on the world level." Since *strategic thinking* is a basic part of the planning process introduced in this series, I can think of no better source for learning the thinking process than one of the world's leading authorities on cognitive thinking.

Goodwin, B. Terence. *Write on the Wall: A How-To Guide for Effective Planning in Groups*. Alexandria, Va.: American Society for Training and Development (ASTD), 1994.

Since I am a strong proponent of the use of a skilled facilitator in the planning process, the title of this book caught my eye at a recent ASTD national conference. It is one of the most concise yet thorough guides to facilitation of the planning process that I have seen. I recommend it to anyone, brand new or experienced, who is charged with the responsibility of facilitating a group planning process.

Hamel, Gary, and Prahalad, C. K. *Competing for the Future: Breakthrough Strategies for Seizing Control of Your Industry and Creating the Markets of Tomorrow*. Boston: Harvard Business School Press, 1994.

One of the most insightful and provocative books to come out in recent years on preparing to make a difference in the marketplace of the future, this book is a wake-up call for managers who still believe that what has worked in the past will continue to produce the desired results in the future. One of the profound changes the authors see as necessary for those companies that expect to be successful in the future is the need to focus more on the development and enhancement of core competencies and less on gaining immediate market share. This is *must* reading for anyone who expects to compete successfully in the future.

Mintzberg, Henry. *The Rise and Fall of Strategic Planning*, New York: Free Press, 1994.

Although this appears to be an overt attack on strategic planning, it is more of a plea to do what is necessary to move an organization forward in meeting the challenges of the future. Mintzberg pulls no punches in assessing many of the accepted strategic planning theories and practices (if nothing else, it is entertaining reading in that respect). The final section of the book, "Planning, Plans, Planners," moves from the critical to the constructive, describing, among other factors, the new roles of planners as finders of strategy, as analysts, and as catalysts. His emphasis on coupling analysis and intuition helped clarify my thinking in drawing the distinctions among strategic thinking, long-range planning, and tactical planning.

Morrisey, George L. *Creating Your Future: Personal Strategic Planning for Professionals*. San Francisco: Berrett-Koehler, 1992.
> This book shows how to apply the principles and techniques of strategic planning to your own career growth, personal life, business development, and financial planning.

Morrisey, George L. *Management by Objectives and Results in the Public Sector* and *Management by Objectives and Results for Business and Industry*. Reading, Mass.: Addison-Wesley, 1976, 1977.
> These two books provide a how-to approach to making the MOR process work for managers in government and in business, respectively.

Morrisey, George L., Below, Patrick J., and Acomb, Betty L. *The Executive Guide to Operational Planning*. San Francisco: Jossey-Bass, 1987.
> This book, together with my prior books on Management by Objectives and Results, provided a foundation for the third book in this series, *A Guide to Tactical Planning*.

Odiorne, George S. *Management by Objectives: A System of Managerial Leadership*. New York: Pitman, 1965.
> George Odiorne was my colleague, mentor, and friend until his untimely passing a few years ago. This book was the one that put MBO on the map and helped make that concept one of the most enduring management "labels" of all time.

Odiorne, George S. *Strategic Management of Human Resources: A Portfolio Approach*. San Francisco: Jossey-Bass, 1984.
> This book is especially helpful for those who are required to analyze human resources in the strategic planning process. George shows how to apply portfolio analysis to human resource management and offers practical approaches for managing and capitalizing on high-performing employees.

Porter, Michael E. *Competitive Strategy: Techniques for Analyzing Industries and Competitors* and *Competitive Advantage: Creating and Sustaining Superior Performance*. New York: Free Press, 1980, 1985.
> These two landmark books provide a wealth of information on approaches and techniques for competitive analysis. They are especially useful for market analysts who are required to come up with the data needed to complete market segment analyses in highly competitive industries.

Ramsey, Jackson E., and Ramsey, Inez L. *Budgeting Basics: How to Survive the Budgeting Crisis*. New York: Franklin Watts, 1985.
> In searching libraries, I found very few books that addressed budgeting in anything other than "accountingese." This one is clearly the exception. It takes a potentially dry subject and puts it into clear, easy-to-read, nonfinan-

cial terms. The authors use a continuing case study throughout that is fun to follow. The chapter "New Department Budgeting" is especially helpful; it provides a good start-to-finish method, including how to make estimates on workload, human resource skills, materials, and operating costs. The book provides everything a nonfinancial manager needs to know, and then some, about what goes into the preparation of budgets.

Redding, John C., and Catalanello, Ralph F. *Strategic Readiness: The Making of the Learning Organization*. San Francisco: Jossey-Bass, 1994.
This book expands on the concept of the learning organization introduced in Peter Senge's *The Fifth Discipline* (New York: Doubleday, 1990). Its main focus is not on individual learning or team learning but on the organization-wide process through which entire firms plan, implement, and modify strategic directions. It moves beyond abstract descriptions of learning organizations and offers numerous illustrations of learning organizations in action.

Ruskin, Arnold M., and Estes, W. Eugene. *What Every Engineer Should Know About Project Management* (2nd ed.). New York: Marcel Dekker, 1995.
Project management is a very precise form of tactical planning, one that is bread and butter for most engineers. Arnie Ruskin has been a friend and colleague for many years. He and coauthor Eugene Estes have written one of the most practical books I have seen on the subject. The chapters on "Control Techniques" and "Risk Management" are especially useful for engineers and managers whose very survival may depend on assessing and controlling costs.

Steiner, George A. *Strategic Planning: What Every Manager Must Know*. New York: Free Press, 1979.
George Steiner's contributions to strategic and long-range planning are legendary. This book provides a comprehensive approach to strategic planning, including a wide variety of analytical techniques. It is especially useful for those wanting an in-depth understanding of the strategic planning process.

Tomasko, Robert M. *Rethinking the Corporation: The Architecture of Change*. New York: Amacom, 1993.
This is a refreshing look at the process of moving an organization from where it is now to where it needs to be, using the logic of the architect. Tomasko's sense of direction for the new corporation is: "It will be a business with few walls. Its structure will minimize barriers between staff thinkers and line doers, between functions and divisions, and between the company and the outside world."

Treacy, Michael, and Wiersema, Fred. *The Discipline of Market Leaders: Choose Your Customers, Narrow Your Focus, Dominate Your Market*. Reading, Mass.: Addison-Wesley, 1995.

The word *focus* is one of the most important words in the planning lexicon. This book brings this message home with a vengeance. The authors have identified three distinct value disciplines: *operational excellence, product leadership*, and *customer intimacy*. Their position, backed by real-world examples, is that companies that are real market leaders select one of these disciplines on which to stake their market reputation, even though they may continue to address the remaining two disciplines. Understanding these three value disciplines and how they work can be a significant step in the formulation of corporate strategy.

Tregoe, Benjamin B., and Zimmerman, John W. *Top Management Strategy: What It Is and How to Make It Work*. New York: Simon & Schuster, 1980; and Tregoe, Benjamin B., Zimmerman, John W., Smith, Ronald A., and Tobia, Peter M. *Vision in Action: Putting a Winning Strategy to Work*. New York: Simon & Schuster, 1989.

The first of these two books introduced the concept of the *driving force* as a powerful tool for determining strategy or strategic direction. It significantly influenced my and my coauthors' interpretation of strategy in our book *The Executive Guide to Strategic Planning*. The second book describes how the Kepner-Tregoe team has expanded and applied their approach to strategy in several well-known organizations, including addressing the perceptions of several managers within those organizations.

Weiss, Alan. *Making It Work: Turning Strategy Into Action Throughout Your Organization*. New York: HarperCollins, 1990.

The focus in this book is on implementation. Alan's premise is that the failure of strategies is most often not the result of poorly conceived strategies but rather the result of poor implementation. In an entertaining manner, he suggests some solid techniques for translating strategic thinking and long-range planning into real-world action.

Index

48; conclusions in, 44, 46; in customer relations, 46–47; defined, 33–34; departmental, 48; examples of, 40, 42–47, 48; functions of, 34; identifying alternative courses of action in, 44, 46, 48; identifying issues in, 34–35, 36–38, 42; importance of, 33; Key Performance Indicators in, 47, 48, 49–54; prioritizing issues in, 35–36, 38–39, 42; steps in, 34–40; summarizing issues in, 36, 39–40, 44; worksheet for, 45. *See also* Issues
Cross-functional coordination/communication, 100
Cross-functional integration, 29, 53
Cross-functional management, 2
Cross-functional planning, 6–7
Customer relations, critical issue analysis in, 46–47
Customer service: controlling, 85; objectives for, 64

D

de Bono, Edward, 122
Departmental critical issue analysis, 48
Departmental roles-and-missions statements, 112–117
Document, planning, 4, 100–102
Drucker, Peter, 27, 120

E

Effectiveness: vs. efficiency, 27; objectives for, 66
Efficiency, vs. effectiveness, 27
Employee development: Key Performance Indicators of, 53; as Key Results Area, 29; objectives for, 65
Employee errors, 87–88
Employee involvement, 3, 100, 105
Engineering department, roles-and-missions statement of, 113–114
Environment, and action plan, 80
Errors, human, 87–88
Estes, W. Eugene, 125
Events: and action plan, 81; unexpected, 87, 103
Executive(s). *See* Chief executive officer; Senior management

Executive Guide to Operational Planning, The, 17

F

Facilitator. *See* Planning process facilitator
Failures, 87
Feedback mechanisms: in action plans, 75; and management controlling, 84, 88–90; and planned information sharing, 96–97
Finances: and action plan, 75, 80; and performance, 29. *See also* Costs
Finnegan, Jerome P., 121
First-line managers, role in planning, 7–8
Focus. *See* Key Results Areas
"Fuzzy ball," 22–23

G

Gaebler, Ted, 121
Goodwin, B. Terence, 123
Governmental agencies, 103–104
Graphs, 89
Group discussion, 39
Growth, objectives for, 65

H

Hall, Dean G., 122
Hamel, Gary, 123
Hammer, Michael, 120
Human error, 87–88

I

Image, organizational: Key Performance Indicators of, 53; as Key Result Area, 29
Incompetency, 87
Individual assignments, 39
Industrial engineering, sample action plan for, 77
Information sharing, 96–98
Interdepartmental relations, objectives for, 66
Involvement: benefits of, 3, 9, 105; resistance to, 4–6, 9
Issues: analyzing, 36, 39, 43–44, 45;